Topps E

PRICE STERN SLOAN

There is a **Topps** BASEBALL CARD BOOK for every major league team. Collect them all or concentrate on your favorites.

Available for all 26 teams!

Topps BASEBALL CARD BOOKS are available wherever books or baseball cards are sold, or may be ordered directly from the publisher. Simply send your check or money order for $9.95 plus $2.00 for shipping and handling to—

PRICE STERN SLOAN
Cash Sales
360 North La Cienega Boulevard
Los Angeles, CA 90048

You'll find books for all 26 major league teams at the **Topps** BOOKS HEADQUARTERS STORE. To locate the HEADQUARTERS nearest you, simply call:

PRICE STERN SLOAN
(800) 421-0892
Calling from CA (800) 227-8801

BASEBALL CARDS

Text by
Larry Schwartz

PRICE STERN SLOAN
Los Angeles

Copyright © 1989 by Topps Chewing Gum, Inc.
Text and statistics Copyright © 1989 by MBKA, Inc.

Published by Price Stern Sloan, Inc.
360 North La Cienega Boulevard, Los Angeles, California 90048

ISBN 0-8431-2467-9

All rights reserved. No part of this publication may be reproduced, stored in a retrieval system, or transmitted, in any form or by any means, electronic, mechanical, photocopying, recording, or otherwise, without prior written permission of the publishers.

Officially licensed by Major League Baseball

Official Licensee

© 1988 MLBPA
© MSA

An MBKA Production

Printed and bound in Hong Kong.

TEAM LEADERS

Toronto Blue Jays Year-by-Year Batting Leaders

Home Runs
1977 - Ron Fairly (19)
1978 - John Mayberry (22)
1979 - John Mayberry (21)
1980 - John Mayberry (30)
1981 - John Mayberry (17)
1982 - Willie Upshaw (21)
1983 - Jesse Barfield, Willie Upshaw (27)
1984 - George Bell (26)
1985 - George Bell (28)
1986 - Jesse Barfield (40)
1987 - George Bell (47)
1988 - Fred McGriff (34)

Runs Batted In
Doug Ault, Ron Fairly (64)
John Mayberry (70)
John Mayberry (74)
John Mayberry (82)
John Mayberry, Lloyd Moseby (43)
Willie Upshaw (75)
Willie Upshaw (104)
Lloyd Moseby (92)
George Bell (95)
Jesse Barfield, George Bell (108)
George Bell (134)
George Bell (97)

Batting Average
Roy Howell (.316)
Roy Howell (.270)
Alfredo Griffin (.287)
Alvis Woods (.300)
Damaso Garcia (.252)
Damaso Garcia (.310)
Lloyd Moseby (.315)
Dave Collins (.308)
Rance Mulliniks (.295)
Tony Fernandez (.310)
Tony Fernandez (.322)
Tony Fernandez (.287)

Toronto Blue Jays Year-by-Year Pitching Leaders

Wins
1977 - Dave Lemanczyk (13)
1978 - Jim Clancy (10)
1979 - Tom Underwood (9)
1980 - Jim Clancy (13)
1981 - Dave Stieb (11)
1982 - Dave Stieb (17)
1983 - Dave Stieb (17)
1984 - Doyle Alexander (17)
1985 - Doyle Alexander (17)
1986 - Jim Clancy (14)
       Mark Eichhorn (14)
       Jimmy Key (14)
1987 - Jimmy Key (17)
1988 - Dave Stieb (16)

Strikeouts
Jerry Garvin (127)
Tom Underwood (140)
Tom Underwood (127)
Jim Clancy (152)
Dave Stieb (89)
Dave Stieb (149)
Dave Stieb (187)
Dave Stieb (198)
Dave Stieb (167)
Mark Eichhorn (166)

Jim Clancy (180)
Dave Stieb (147)

Earned Run Average
Pete Vuckovich (3.47)
Jim Clancy (4.09)
Tom Underwood (3.69)
Jim Clancy (3.30)
Dave Stieb (3.19)
Dave Stieb (3.25)
Dave Stieb (3.04)
Dave Stieb (2.83)
Dave Stieb (2.48)
Mark Eichhorn (1.72)

Jimmy Key (2.76)
Dave Stieb (3.04)

Toronto Blue Jays Award Winners

Player of the Year
1977 - Bob Bailor
1978 - Bob Bailor
1979 - Alfredo Griffin
1980 - John Mayberry
1981 - Dave Stieb
1982 - Damaso Garcia
1983 - Lloyd Moseby
1984 - Dave Collins
1985 - Jesse Barfield
1986 - Jesse Barfield
1987 - George Bell

Pitcher of the Year
Dave Lemanczyk
Jim Clancy, Victor Cruz
Tom Underwood
Jim Clancy
Dave Stieb
Dave Stieb
Dave Stieb
Doyle Alexander
Dennis Lamp
Mark Eichhorn
Jimmy Key

Rookie of the Year
Bob Bailor
Victor Cruz
Alfredo Griffin
Damaso Garcia
—
Jesse Barfield
Jim Acker
Tony Fernandez
—
Mark Eichhorn
Jeff Musselman

Most Improved Player
Alan Ashby
Rick Cerone
Alvis Woods
Joey McLaughlin
Jim Clancy
Lloyd Moseby
Dave Collins
Dennis Lamp
Rick Leach
Lloyd Moseby

Toronto Blue Jays Grand Slam Home Runs

6-27-77 Hector Torres
5-07-78 Rick Bosetti
7-31-78 Rico Carty
7-03-79 Roy Howell
8-27-79 Roy Howell
9-07-79 Rico Carty
4-26-80 Otto Velez
4-24-82 Jesse Barfield
5-01-83 Barry Bonnell
6-05-83 Buck Martinez
9-11-83 Willie Upshaw
4-20-84 Lloyd Moseby
6-23-85 Ernie Whitt
7-09-85 George Bell
8-02-85 George Bell
5-22-86 Ernie Whitt
6-20-86 George Bell
8-31-86 Lloyd Moseby
6-11-87 George Bell
6-23-87 Willie Upshaw
8-27-87 George Bell

Toronto Blue Jays Inside-The-Park Home Runs

8-21-77 Doug Rader
7-09-79 Alvis Woods
8-28-79 Alfredo Griffin
9-17-80 Roy Howell
4-25-81 Lloyd Moseby
6-07-82 Willie Upshaw
4-14-83 Willie Upshaw
5-25-83 Jorge Orta
5-30-83 Lloyd Moseby
9-14-83 Barry Bonnell
6-06-84 George Bell
8-10-84 Tony Fernandez
6-12-86 Kelly Gruber

Toronto Blue Jays One-Hitters

4-24-79 Dave Lemanczyk (at Texas)
8-27-79 Phil Huffman (vs. A's)
5-30-82 Jim Gott (6 innings)
Roy Lee Jackson (3 innings) at Baltimore
9-28-82 Jim Clancy (vs. Twins)
5-14-83 Luis Leal (5 innings)
Roy Lee Jackson (4 innings) at Cleveland
5-22-86 Jimmy Key (at Chicago)

1977

The American League expanded to 14 teams for the 1977 season with the addition of Toronto and Seattle. The Toronto franchise was awarded in March 1976 to a group headed by the Labatt Brewing Co. at a cost of $7 million. Team directors selected the nickname "Blue Jays" from more than 4,000 names and 30,000 entries in a "Name the Team" contest. In November, $5.25 million was shelled out for 30 players at $175,000 each in the expansion draft in which the Blue Jays and Mariners selected from the lists of the 12 established A.L. teams. The Blue Jays chose shortstop Bob Bailor from the Baltimore organization with their first selection. Under the front-office wisdom of Peter Bavasi and Pat Gillick, the Blue Jays went with youth rather than dealing for veterans. The decision cost the team some victories the first few years but in the long run it was beneficial. Within a decade, the Blue Jays not only were contenders but were in the playoffs. Pitcher Jim Clancy (chosen from the Rangers), catcher Ernie Whitt (Red Sox) and third baseman Garth Iorg (Yankees) are original Blue Jays who still were around a decade later.

The manager was Roy Hartsfield, who had been in the game for 34 years but had never managed in the majors before. His club was 30-47 on the morning of July 4 but then went 24-60 to finish with the worst record in the major leagues at 54-107. The Blue Jays came in last in the seven-team A.L. East, 45½ games behind the Yankees.

There were bright spots. In the opener, Doug Ault homered in his first two at-bats to lead Toronto to a 9-5 win over the White Sox before an SRO crowd of 44,649 which braved snow and freezing temperature to come to 43,737-seat Exhibition Stadium. On Sept. 10, the Blue Jays humiliated the A.L. champion Yankees 19-3, the most runs scored against them in more than half a century. Third baseman Roy Howell, obtained in May from Texas, knocked in nine runs as he went five-for-six, including two home runs.

Howell led Toronto with a .316 average in 96 games while Bailor, switched to centerfield, batted .310. Ron Fairly led the team with 19 homers and his 64 RBIs, which tied him for the most with Ault, and was two more than outfielder Otto Velez knocked in. Dave Lemanczyk (13-16) and Jerry Garvin (10-18) were the top pitchers. The team drew 1,701,052, a record for an expansion team in its first season.

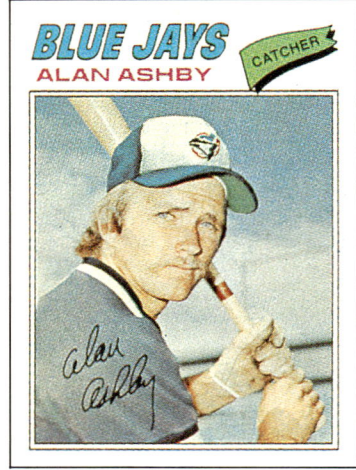
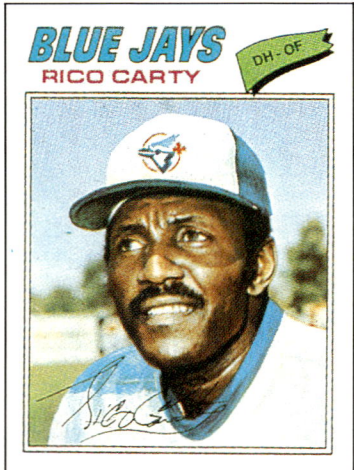

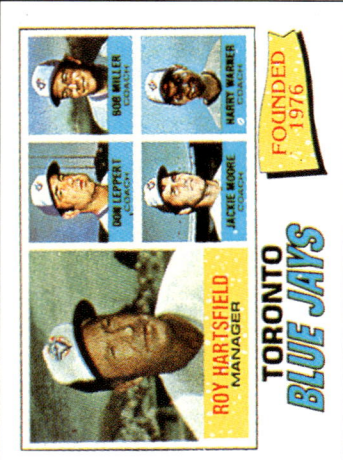

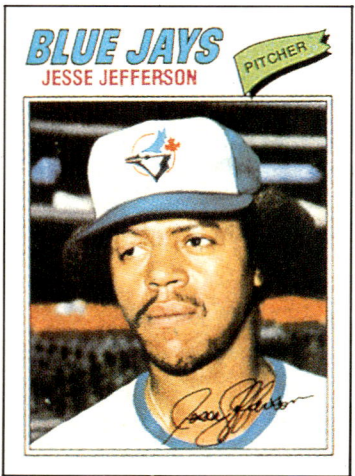

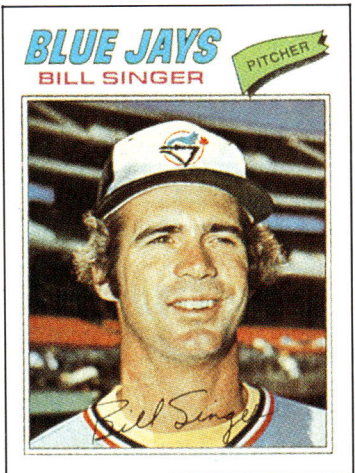

1978

On June 26, the Blue Jays exploded for 24 runs and 24 hits in a 24-10 rout of the Orioles. For the rest of the season, runs were more difficult to come by. The Blue Jays scored the second fewest runs (590) in the major leagues in compiling a 59-102 record, which left them in last place, 40 games behind the Yankees. A nine-game losing streak in June included three consecutive doubleheader losses. The Blue Jays straightened themselves out in August, winning 16 of 30 games, but then ended the season by losing 22 of their final 26 games.

Designated hitter Rico Carty was leading the team in homers (20) and RBIs (68) when he was traded to Oakland for designated hitter Willie Horton and minor league pitcher Phil Huffman on Aug. 15. Two days after the season ended, Carty was brought back to Toronto, purchased from the A's. In Carty's absence, first baseman John Mayberry, bought by the Blue Jays from Kansas City three days before the opener, led the team with 22 home runs and 70 RBIs.

Bob Bailor, shifted from centerfield to rightfield, had his batting average drop 46 points to .264 but he was the most difficult player in the league to fan. He struck out just 21 times in 621 at-bats. Alan Ashby, who shared the catching chores with Rick Cerone (.223), raised his average 51 points to .261. After the season, he was traded to Houston for three players, the best of whom was pitcher Mark Lemongello. Second baseman Dave McKay, though he batted just .238, had the team's longest hitting streak of the season—16 games.

Jim Clancy was Toronto's only double-figure winner as he went 10-12 with a 4.08 ERA. Rookie Victor Cruz, recalled in June, was the big man in the bullpen with a 7-3 record, 9 saves, 1.72 ERA and 51 strikeouts in 47 innings. Jerry Garvin (4-12) had a 10-game losing streak for the second straight year.

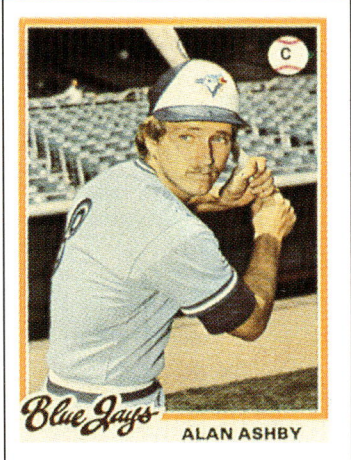
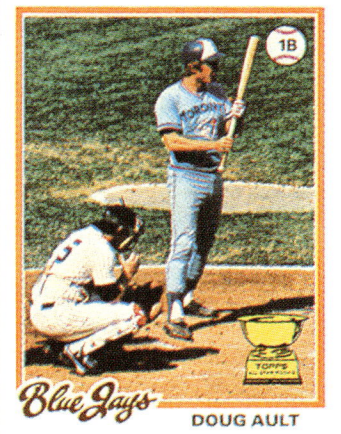

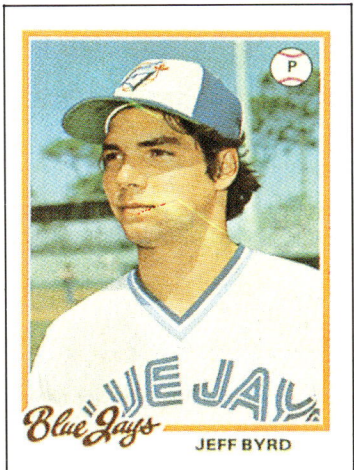

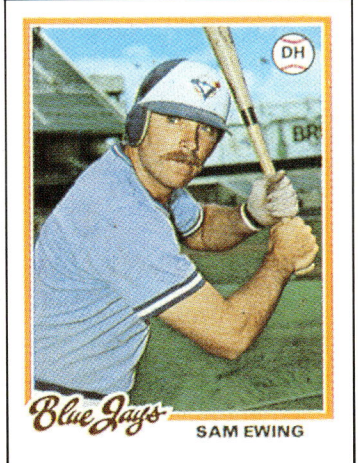

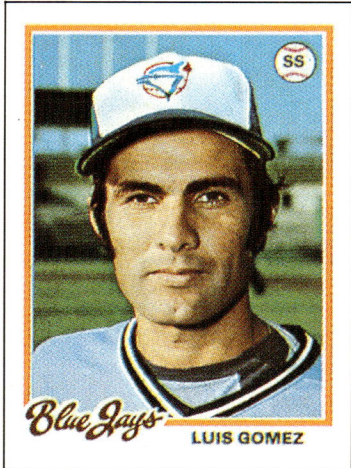

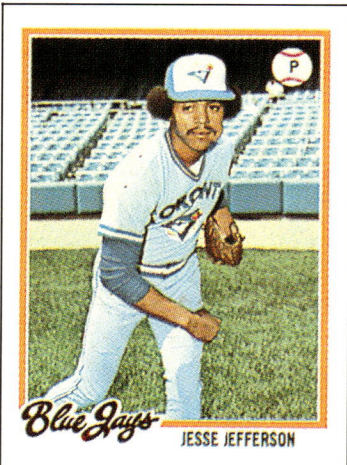

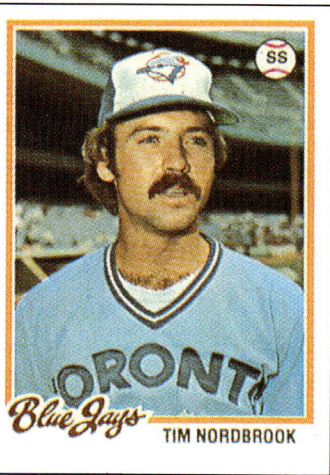
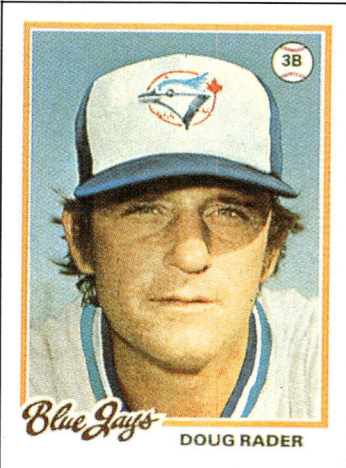

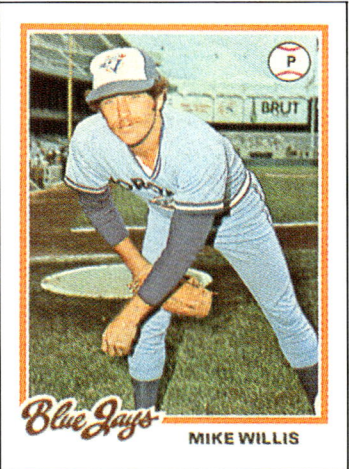

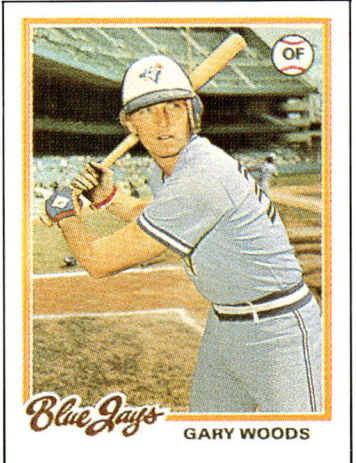

1979

Twice Toronto pitchers were fortunate to get three outs on one pitch. But triple plays don't come that frequently and Toronto pitchers had more trouble getting other outs. Their 4.82 ERA was the highest in the majors and helps explain why the Blue Jays had the worst record in the majors at 53-109. They finished last, 50½ games behind the Orioles, and on the final day Roy Hartsfield resigned as manager.

Shortstop Alfredo Griffin, acquired the previous December in a trade with the Indians for Victor Cruz, started slowly, hitting .082 the first three weeks. But the switch-hitter ended hot, batting .347 in September and being named the A.L. Player of the Month. He received a bigger honor after the season when he was voted co-Rookie of the Year with Minnesota infielder John Castino. Griffin led the Blue Jays in batting (.287), runs (81), steals (21) ad triples (10).

John Mayberry, who hit .274, led the Blue Jays with 21 homers and 74 RBIs. Roy Howell, a .247 batter, had 15 homers and 72 RBIs. Otto Velez also hit 15 homers. Danny Ainge, a basketball standout at Brigham Young University, decided to try baseball. After being promoted from Syracuse in May, he was given the second-base job. However, he hit only .237 in 87 games.

None of the 19 pitchers Toronto used had a winning record. Southpaw Tom Underwood lost his first nine decisions before winning nine of his final 16 to go 9-16. Rookie righthander Dave Stieb, a converted outfielder, tied for the second most wins (8-8, 4.33 ERA) despite not being called up from Syracuse until the season was almost half over. Phil Huffman (6-18, 5.77 ERA) led the league in losses while Mark Lemongello was 1-9 with a 6.29 ERA when he was finally sent down to Syracuse. Huffman's best moment came when he one-hit Oakland. Dave Lemanczyk also pitched a one-hitter.

On Nov. 1, the Blue Jays solved their second-base problems when they obtained Damaso Garcia—along with Chris Chambliss and Paul Mirabella—from the Yankees for Underwood, Rick Cerone and Ted Wilborn. A month later, Chambliss was sent to Atlanta as part of a five-player trade in which the Blue Jays received outfielder Barry Bonnell and pitcher Joey McLaughlin.

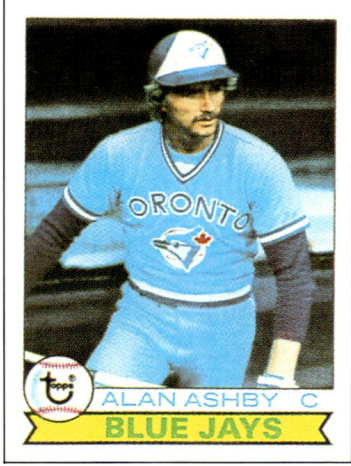

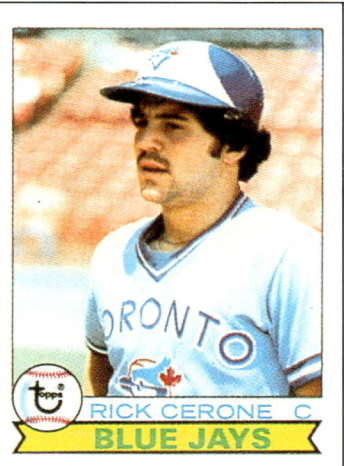

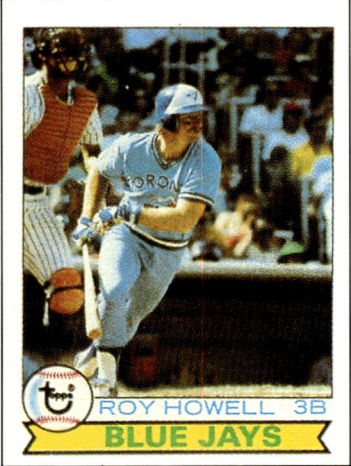

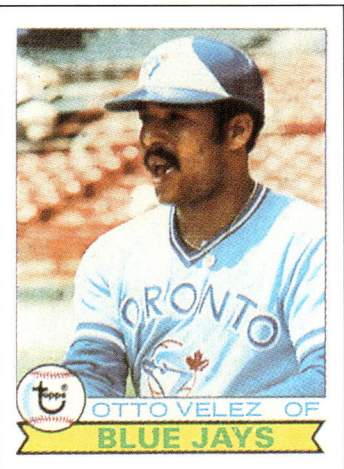

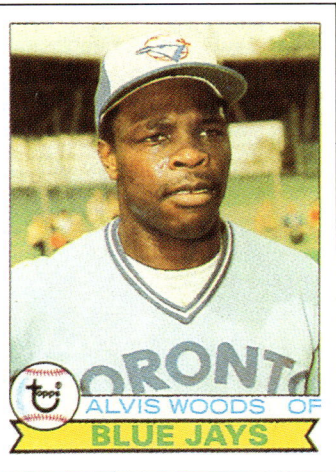
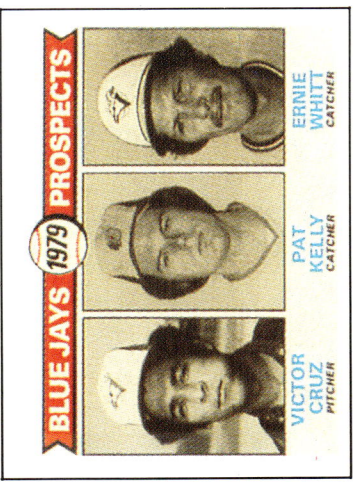

1980

Bobby Mattick, at age 64, became the oldest major league manager to start a season. His only previous managerial experience was in rookie and instructional leagues. He had been the club's director of player development and top scout. Under his guidance, the Blue Jays were 30-30 through June 18 before fading. Still, their 67-95 record was a 14-game improvement over 1979 and it was the first time the Blue Jays didn't lose in three digits. However, last place remained their property and they finished 36 games behind the Yankees.

Righthanders Jim Clancy and Dave Stieb were developing into two of the better pitchers in the league. Clancy had a 13-16 record with a 3.30 ERA. Stieb started off 10-6 before slumping. He finished 12-15 with a 3.70 ERA and pitched four of Toronto's nine shutouts.

Otto Velez had a day to remember on May 4. He became the first Blue Jay to hit three home runs in a game, accomplishing this feat in the first game of a doubleheader against Cleveland. He hit a two-run homer, a grand slam and then a solo homer in the 10th inning to win the game 9-8. In the nightcap, he hit another home run, tying the A.L. record for most homers in a doubleheader (four). Velez had 10 RBIs for the day as the Blue Jays swept. For the season, Velez hit .269 with 20 homers and 62 RBIs in 104 games. The designated hitter missed the last 36 games after suffering a fractured cheekbone in an automobile accident.

John Mayberry led the Blue Jays with 30 homers and 82 RBIs. Leftfielder Al Woods was the top hitter at .300. He missed several weeks with a torn right calf muscle and played in just 109 games. Alfredo Griffin tied with the Royals' Willie Wilson for the most triples in the majors (15). He had the team's longest batting streak of the season (19 games) and hit .254. Rookie second baseman Damaso Garcia was impressive, batting .278, second highest on the Blue Jays. However, he walked just 12 times.

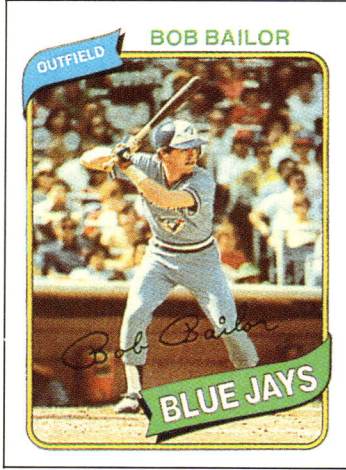
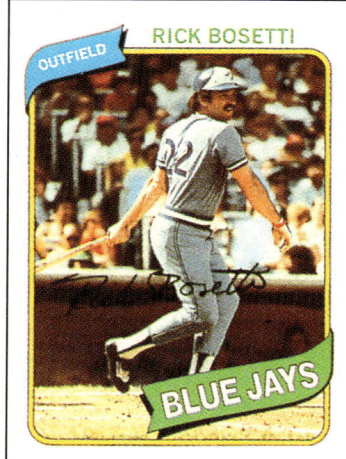
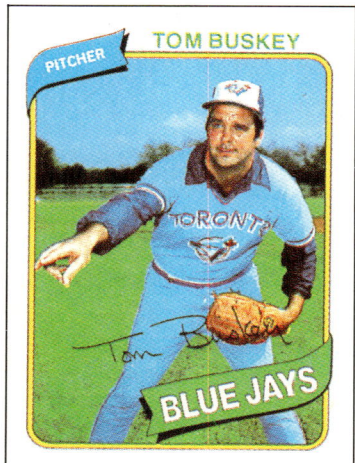
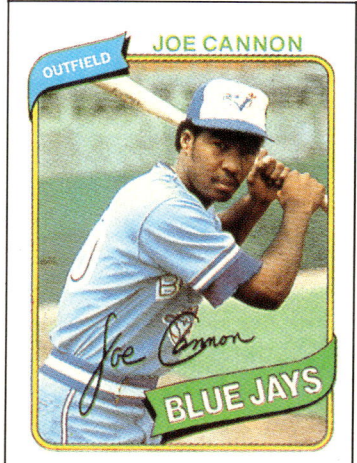

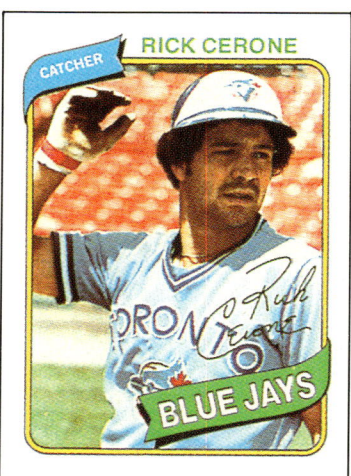
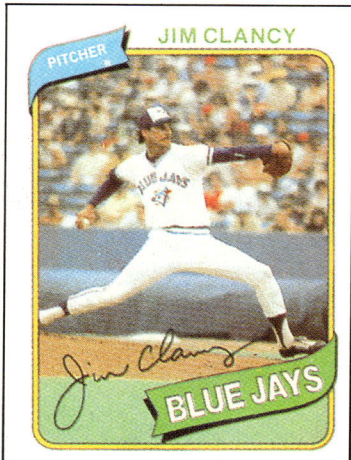
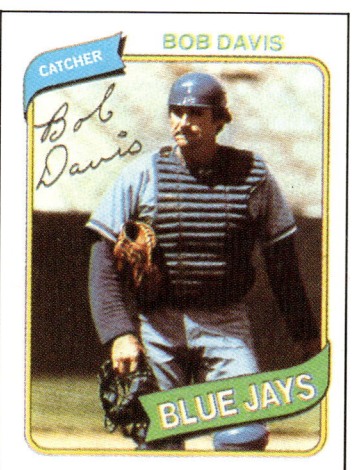

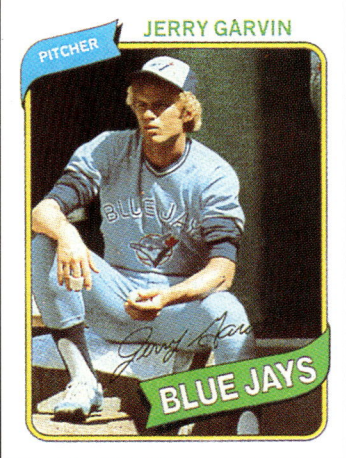

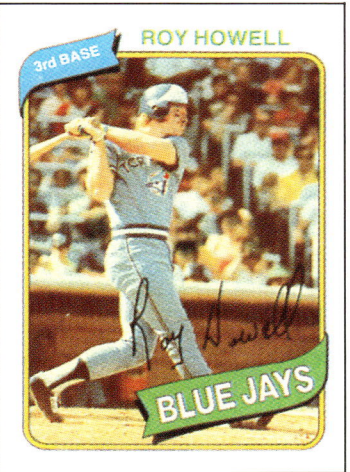

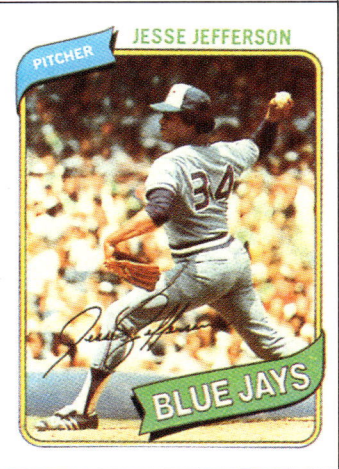
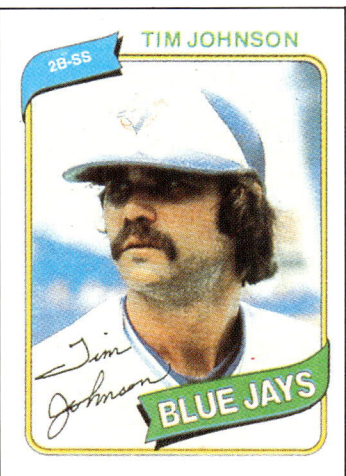

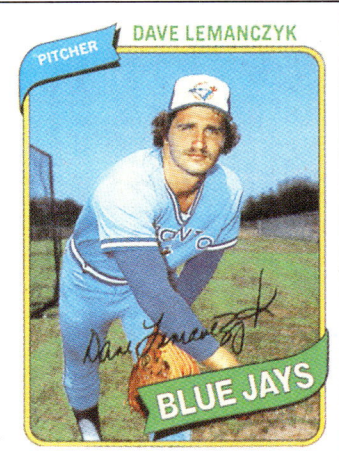

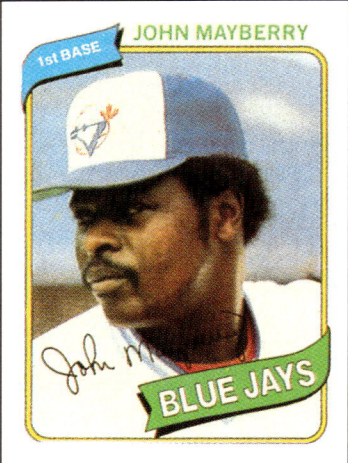
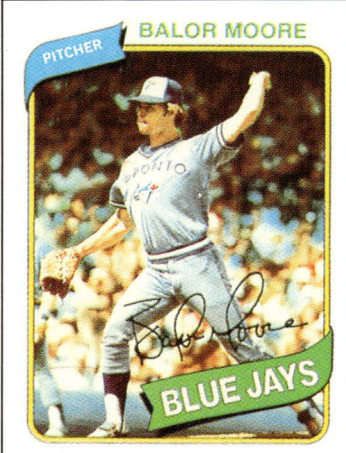
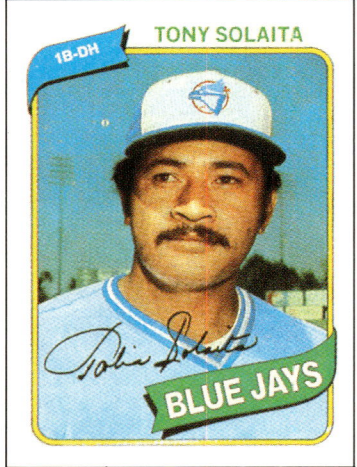
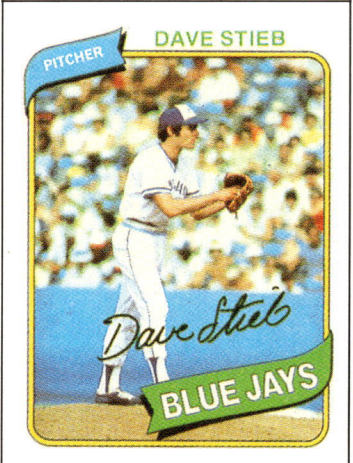
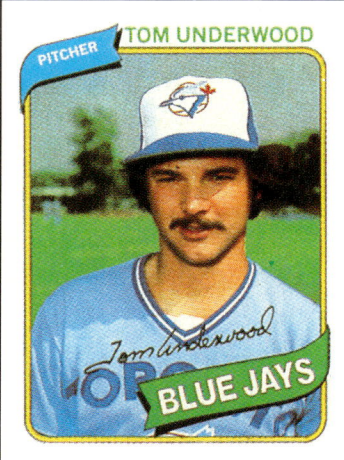
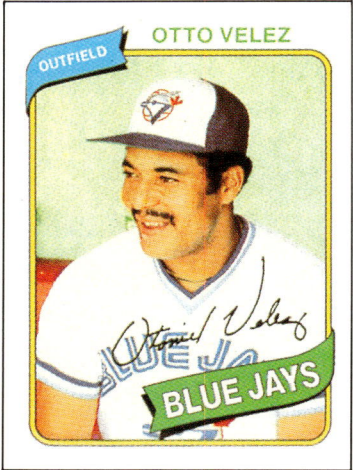
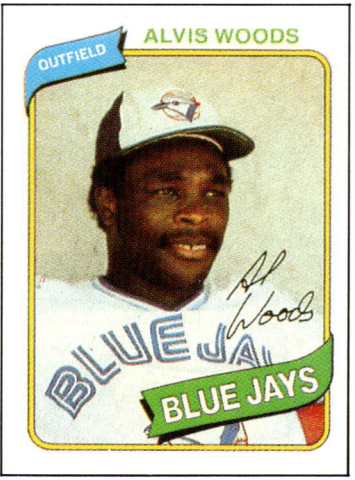

1981

The Blue Jays were on an 11-game losing streak when a players' strike halted the season after games of June 11. The strike caused the season to be divided into two sessions and the Blue Jays' record in the first was 16-42, putting them in last place, 19 games behind the Yankees. When play resumed on Aug. 10, the Blue Jays performed better. They won seven of their first 11 games and were 19-18 with 11 games left. However, they lost nine of those games and fell into last place with a 21-27 record, but just 7½ games behind the Brewers.

The big problem was a lack of hitting. The Blue Jays were shut out 20 times in 106 games. They were last in the majors in batting average (.226) and runs scored (329). Alfredo Griffin had his worst season, batting just .209. Danny Ainge, who missed most of spring training because he was starring for Brigham Young in the NCAA basketball playoffs, was given the third-base job but couldn't handle it. He batted only .187 in 86 games. After the season, he decided he'd rather play basketball. He was released from his baseball contract when the Boston Celtics, who drafted him, compensated the Blue Jays. John Mayberry led Toronto in home runs with 17 and his 43 RBIs tied him for the lead with second-year centerfielder Lloyd Moseby. A hot second half raised Damaso Garcia's average to a team-high .252. He also led the Blue Jays in steals with 13.

Dave Stieb was the only Toronto pitcher with more than one victory to have a winning record (11-10). By winning five of his last six decisions he became the first Toronto starter ever to have a winning mark. He had a 3.18 ERA. Joey McLaughlin became the first Blue Jay to get 10 saves. He reduced his ERA from 4.50 in 1980 to 2.85.

Three days after the season ended, Bobby Mattick stepped down as manager and became executive coordinator, baseball operations. In November, Peter Bavasi resigned as president and chief operating officer.

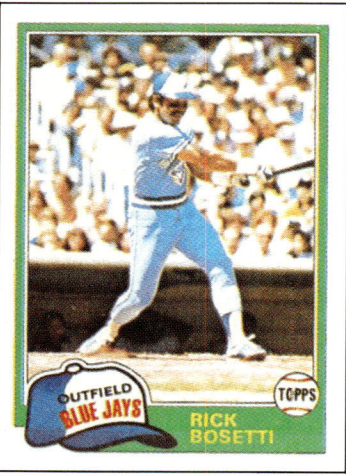

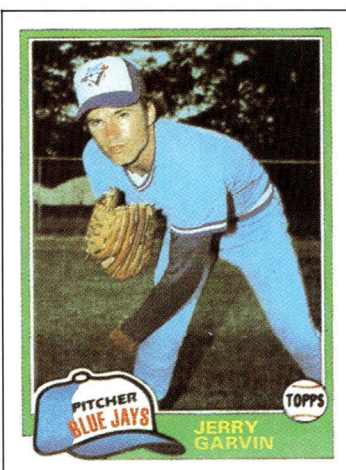

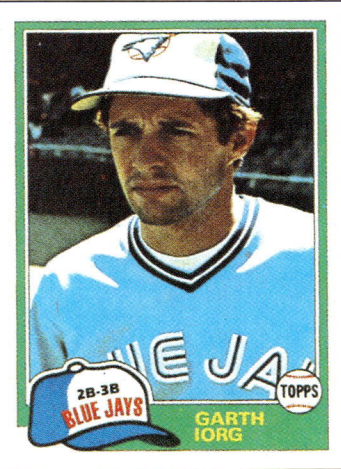

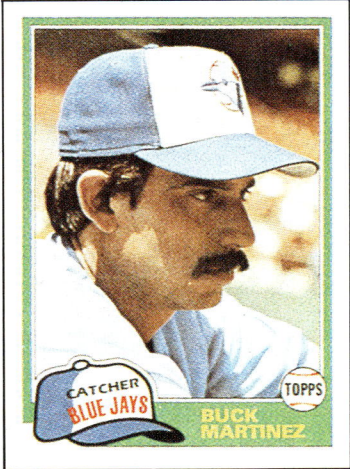

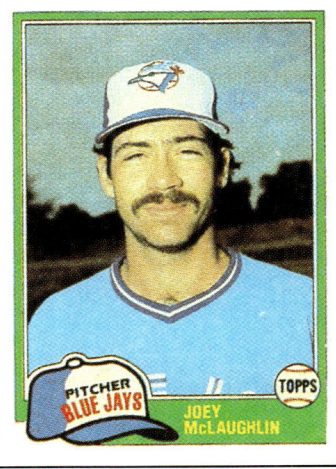

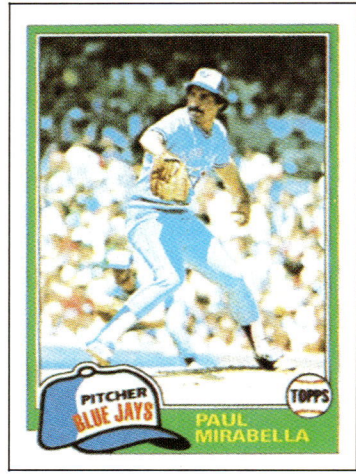

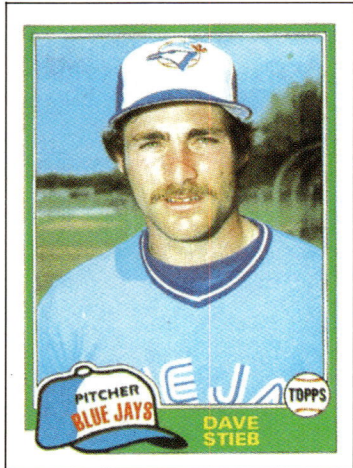

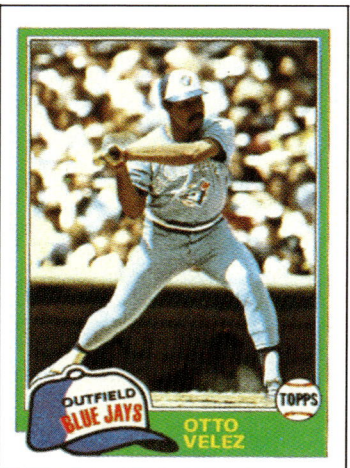

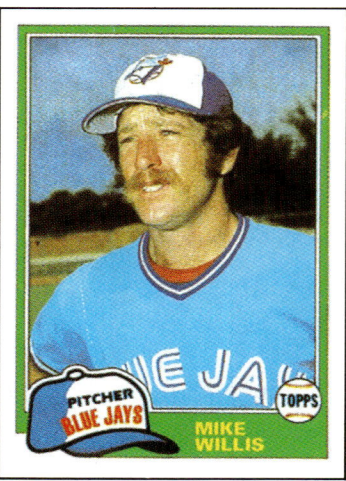

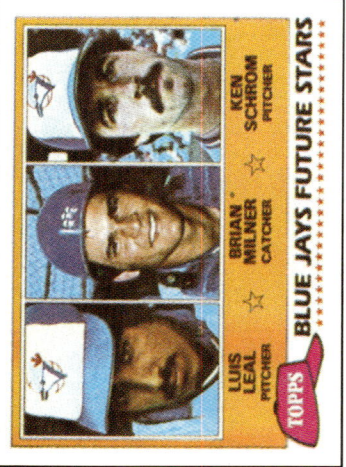

1982

Bobby Cox, who had managed the Atlanta Braves from 1978 through 1981, was the new pilot. He platooned players at several positions and used his bench extensively. As a result the Blue Jays improved to 78-84, tying with the Indians for sixth place, 17 games behind the Brewers. It was the fewest games behind for a last-place club in the A.L. since divisional play started in 1969. For the first time, the Blue Jays had a winning record at home (44-37).

Willie Upshaw, who had been drafted from the Yankee organization in 1977, took over from John Mayberry at first base and led the team in homers (21), RBIs (75) and game-winning RBIs (14). Rookie righthanded hitter Jesse Barfield, who platooned in rightfield, was second on the team with 18 homers (15 off lefthanders) and 58 RBIs. The third-base platoon of Garth Iorg and Rance Mulliniks combined for 71 RBIs while the catching platoon of Ernie Whitt and Buck Martinez accounted for 21 home runs. Leadoff hitter Damaso Garcia had four batting streaks of at least 12 games on his way to hitting a team-high .310. He also led the Blue Jays in runs (89) and steals (54). Alfredo Griffin, playing all 162 games, led A.L. shortstops in total chances (823) and for the first time made fewer than 30 errors (26).

Dave Stieb led the league in complete games (19), innings (288⅓) and shutouts (five). He became the first Toronto pitcher to win 17 games—he lost 14—and posted a 3.25 ERA, which was fifth best in the league. Jim Clancy had a 16-14 record and 3.71 ERA. He led the majors in starts with 40. His best performance came in his final start when he retired the first 24 Twins before Randy Bush led off the ninth with a broken-bat single. Clancy finished with a one-hitter. Dale Murray was the key man in the bullpen (8-7, 11 saves, 3.16 ERA).

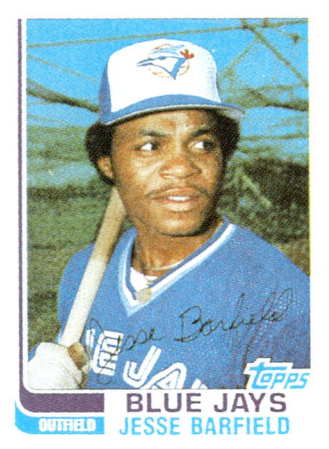

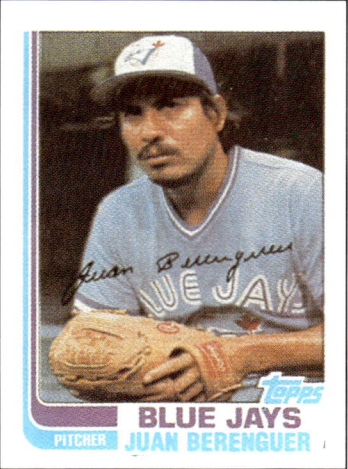
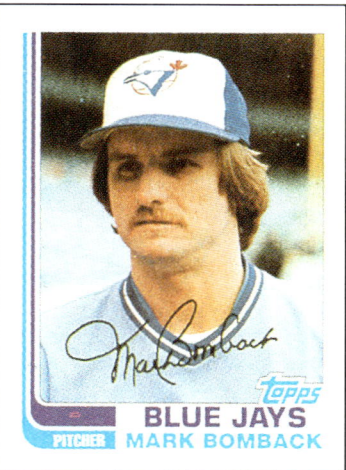

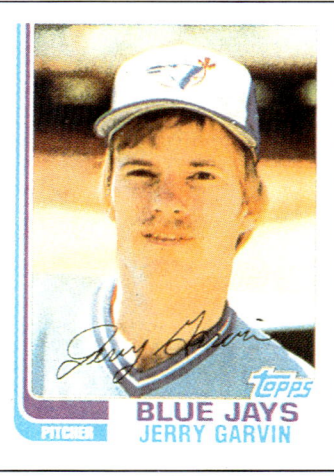

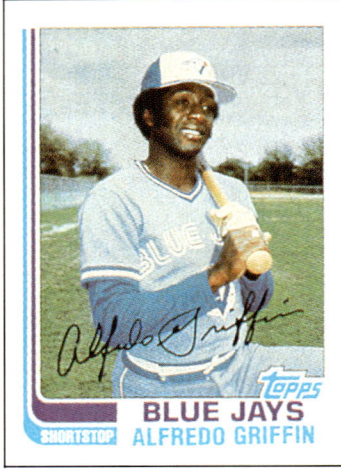

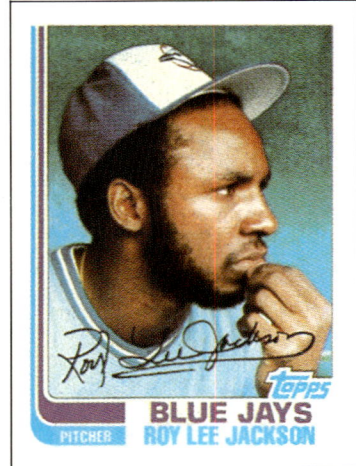
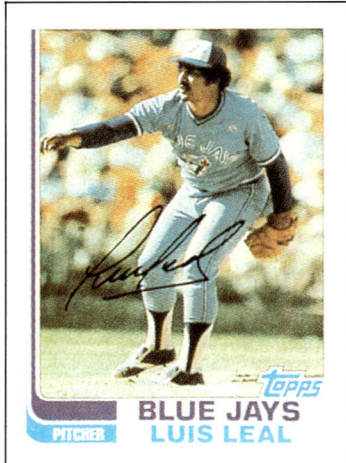

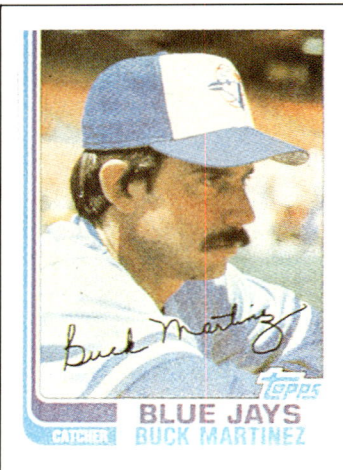

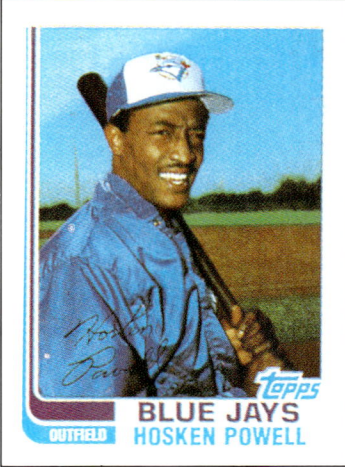

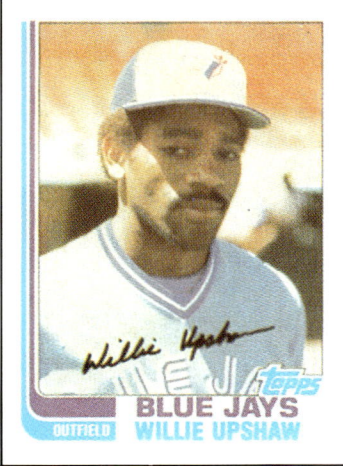

 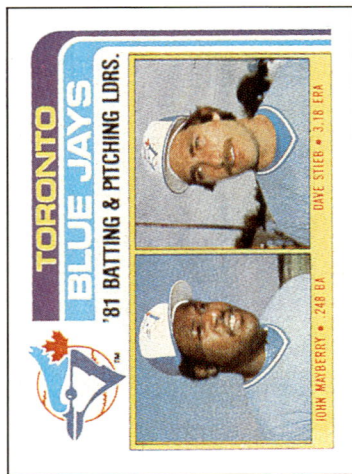 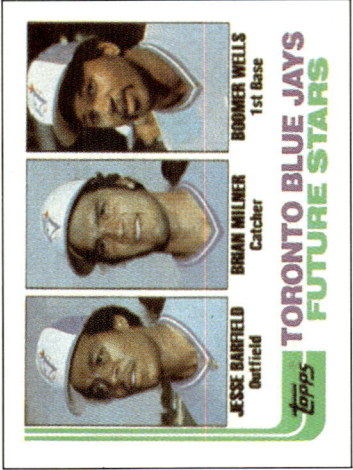

1983

The Blue Jays found out what it was like to be in first place. They spent five weeks there, and were in that position as late as late July. While dog days in August (15-19) cost them a chance at the division title, the Blue Jays still were proud of their first winning season (89-73). They came in fourth, nine games behind the Orioles.

Their hitting was superb. With four .300 hitters, they led the majors in batting average (.277) and were second in runs (795, five fewer than the White Sox) and second in homers (167, one fewer than the Orioles). Barry Bonnell, a platoon outfielder, led the Blue Jays with a .318 average in 377 at-bats. Lloyd Moseby hit .315 (which remains the team record for players who qualified for the batting title) and became the first Blue Jay to score 100 runs (104). He also stole 27 bases. Damaso Garcia hit .307 and tied with outfielder Dave Collins for the team lead in steals with 31. Garcia and Moseby both hit in 21 consecutive games, a Toronto record. Willie Upshaw was the fourth .300 man at .306. He also was the first Blue Jay to drive home 100 runs (104) and tied with Jesse Barfield for the team high in home runs with 27. Designated hitters Cliff Johnson and Jorge Orta combined for 32 home runs and 114 RBIs. Catchers Ernie Whitt and Buck Martinez totaled 27 homers and 89 RBIs.

Dave Stieb started 8-2 on the way to a 17-12 season. Besides leading the Toronto staff in victories, he also was first in shutouts (four), complete games (14) and ERA (3.04, third best in the league). Jim Clancy (15-11, 3.91 ERA) and Luis Leal (13-12, 4.31) did competent jobs as the Nos. 2 and 3 starters. Randy Moffitt, a free agent signed before the season, was the most dependable reliever (6-2, 10 saves, 3.77 ERA).

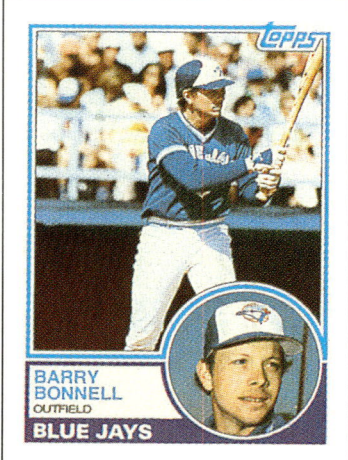

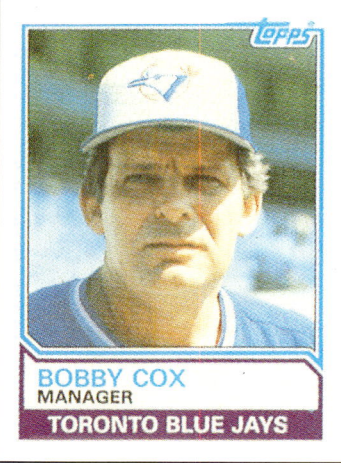

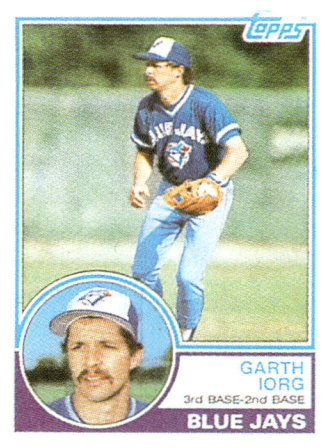

 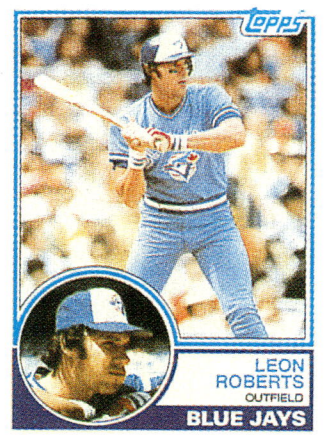 

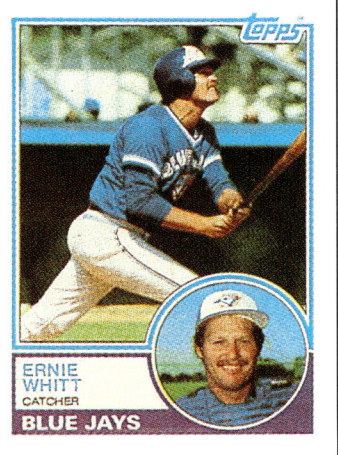
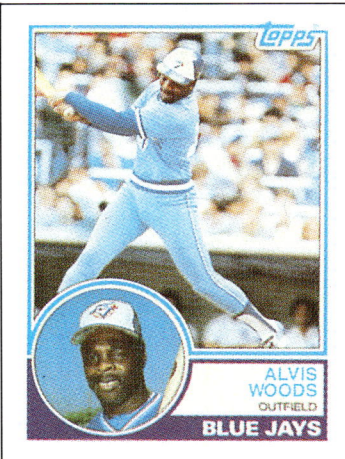
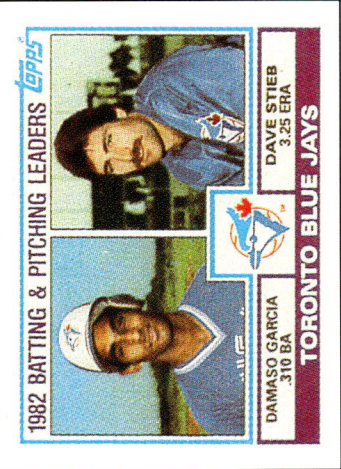

1984

Four weeks into the season, the Blue Jays took over second place, a position they would never relinquish. On June 6, they still had visions of a division title despite the red-hot start of the Tigers. The Blue Jays were 36-17 and only 3½ games behind. But then they played three games below .500 the rest of the way and settled to finish a distant second (15 games behind Detroit) with their 89-73 record. The Blue Jays were especially proficient in one-run games, at one stretch winning 19 consecutive such contests. They led the league in steals with 193 (with Dave Collins getting a club-record 60, Damaso Garcia 46 and Lloyd Moseby 39) and were third in the majors in batting with their .273 average. They had their biggest inning ever when they exploded for 11 runs in the ninth against Seattle. For the first time, they drew more than two million fans (2,110,009) to Exhibition Stadium.

The Blue Jays gained an additional booming bat with the emergence of George Bell. The outfielder led the team with 26 home runs, knocked in 87 runs, batted .292, and hit 39 doubles (third most in the league). Moseby (.280) led the team with 92 RBIs and tied with Collins for the league lead in triples with 15. Willie Upshaw hit .278 with 19 homers and 84 RBIs. Rance Mulliniks, the lefthanded-hitting part of the third-base platoon, led the team with a .324 average in 343 at-bats. Cliff Johnson set a major league record with his 19th career pinch-hit home run. Dave Stieb was outstanding again, going 16-8 with a 2.83 ERA and 198 strikeouts, both second in the league. He also led the A.L. in innings pitched (267). Doyle Alexander, who won his last seven decisions in 1983, picked right up and was the team's top winner at 17-6. He set a Toronto record with his .739 winning percentage. His ERA was 3.13. Jim Clancy, who tied for the league-lead in starts with 36, had a subpar season (13-15, 5.12 ERA). Luis Leal started 12-2, but won only one of his final seven decisions to finish 13-8.

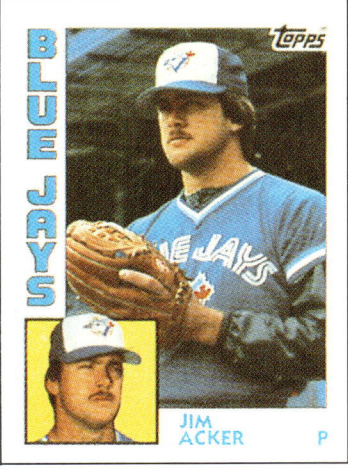

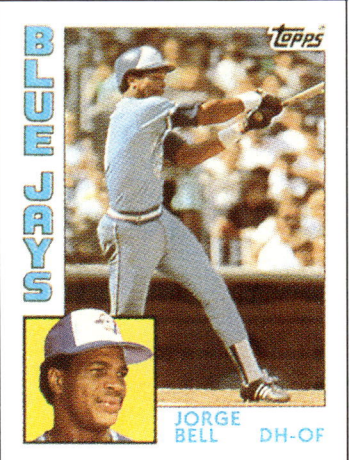
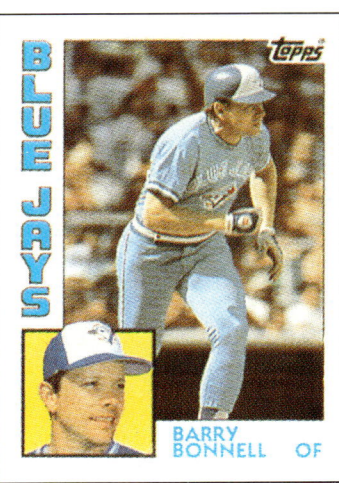

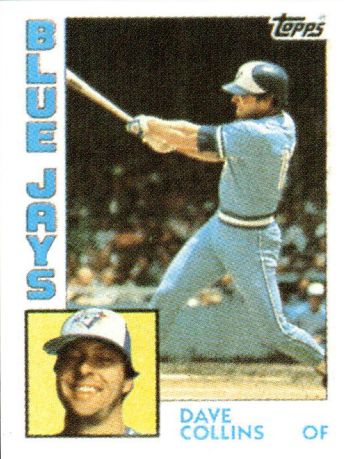

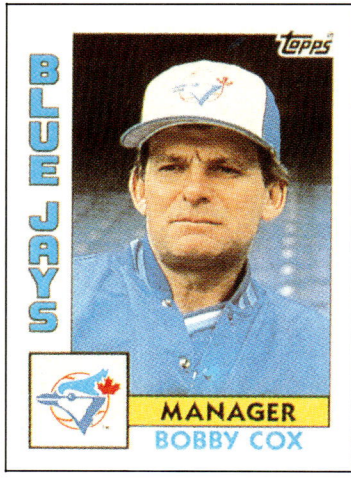
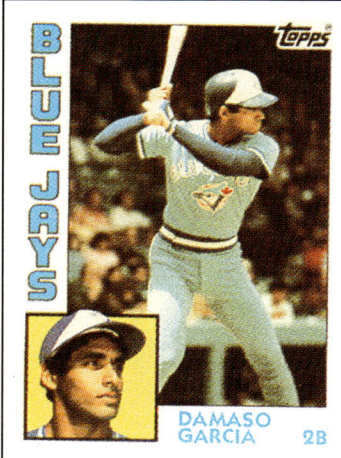

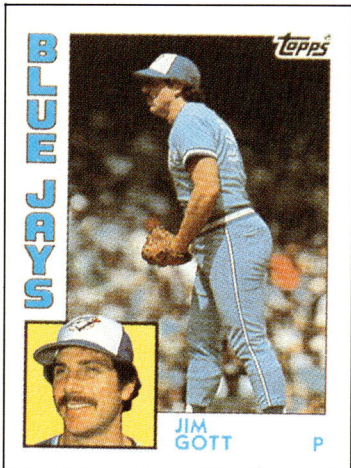

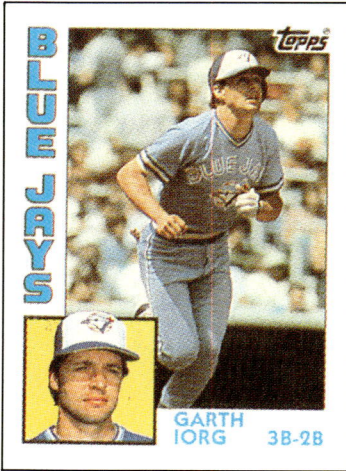
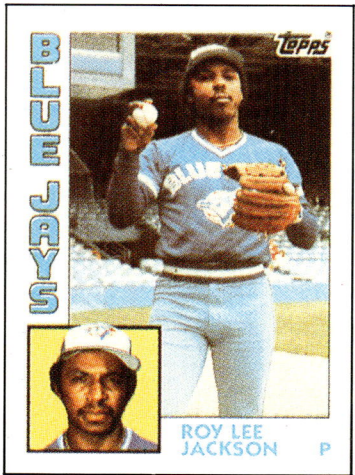
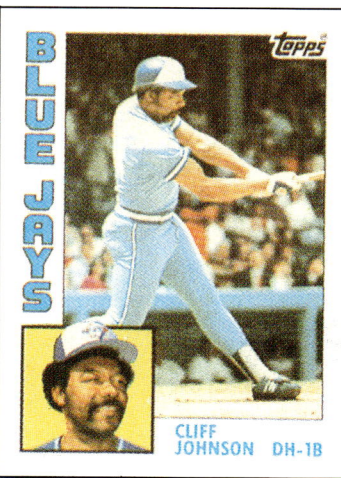
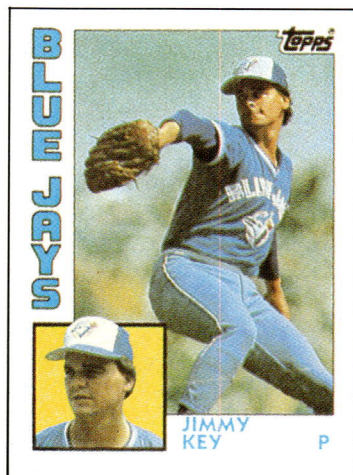

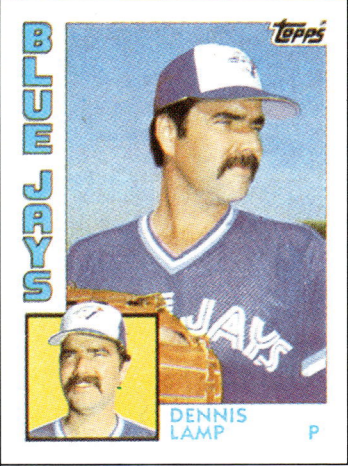
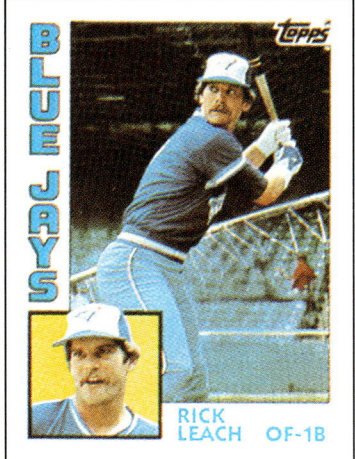

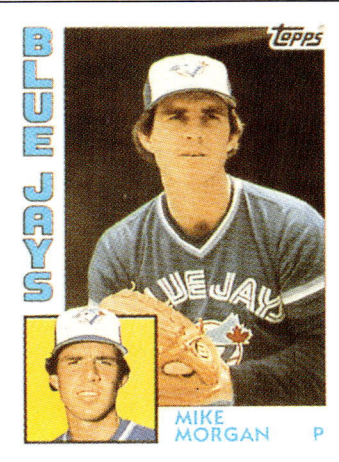

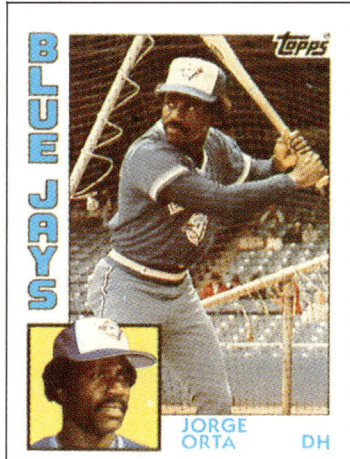
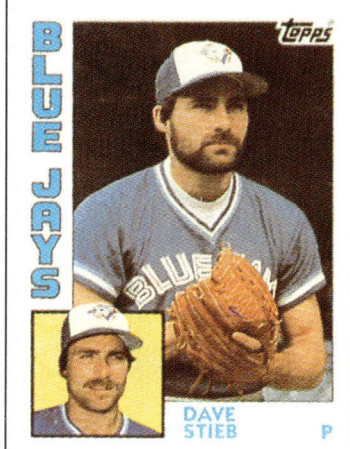
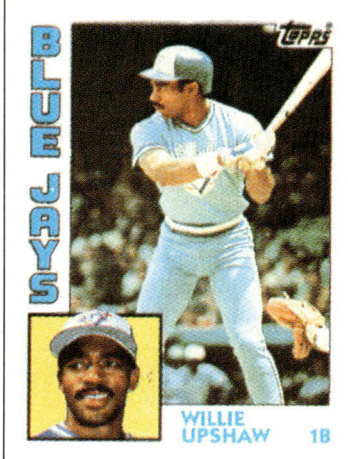
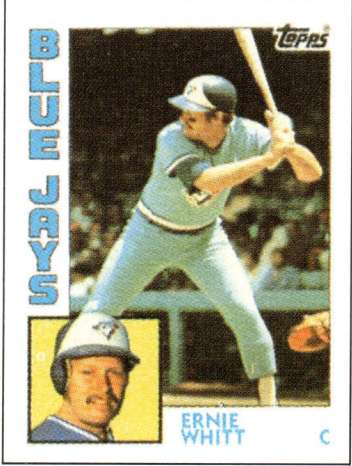
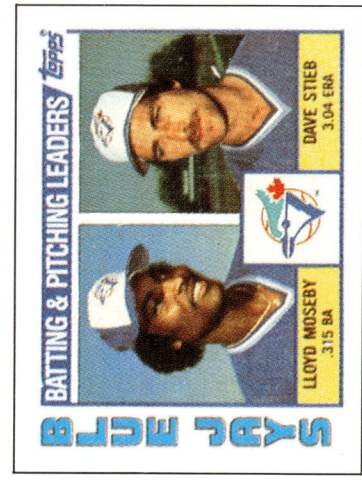

1985

The Blue Jays won their first division championship, finishing with a 99-62 record, two games ahead of the Yankees. They took over sole possession of first place for good on May 20. For a while, it appeared the Blue Jays might win easily, but then the Yankees rallied. They closed the gap to 1½ games on Sept. 12 by beating the Blue Jays. But Bobby Cox's club won the last three games of the series and went on to the title, clinching the division by beating the Yankees on the next-to-last day of the season. Unfortunately for the Blue Jays, this was the first year of the four-of-seven playoffs (instead of three-of-five). They won the first two games against the Royals and three of the first four. But Kansas City came back to win the final three games and win the pennant.

Jesse Barfield, for the first time playing fulltime in rightfield, hit .289 with 27 homers, 84 RBIs, a team-high 94 runs and 22 stolen bases. With his rifle arm he also led major league outfielders in assists with 22. Leftfielder George Bell led the Blue Jays in homers (28) and RBIs (95). He hit .275 and stole 21 bases. The third member of the outfielder—Lloyd Moseby—was down to .259 but hit 18 homers with 71 RBIs and led the team with 37 steals.

With the offseason trade of Alfredo Griffin, Dave Collins and cash to the A's for Bill Caudill, Tony Fernandez became the regular shortstop. He was no disappointment, covering plenty of ground in the field and hitting .289. His keystone partner, Damaso Garcia, hit .282, stole 28 bases and knocked in a career-high 65 runs, a high total for a leadoff hitter. Ernie Whitt had career bests of 19 homers and 64 RBIs. Buck Martinez made the play of the season, getting a DP July 9 by tagging two Mariners at the plate, the second while on his back with a broken leg. He was sidelined for the rest of the season.

The Blue Jays led the A.L. in ERA (3.29) with Dave Stieb winning the individual title at 2.48. He pitched better than his 14-13 record indicates. Jimmy Key (14-6), the first lefthanded Toronto starter to win a game since 1980, was fourth in the A.L. in ERA (3.00). Doyle Alexander was the top winner (17-10, 3.45 ERA). Middle reliever Dennis Lamp went 11-0. Caudill was a bust in the bullpen (4-6, 2.99 ERA, none of his 14 saves after Aug. 3) and Tom Henke, brought up from Syracuse in late July, became the stopper. He had 13 saves in 15 save situations and had a 2.03 ERA in 28 appearances.

The team drew a record 2,468,925 fans. After the season, Cox quit as manager to become GM of the Braves.

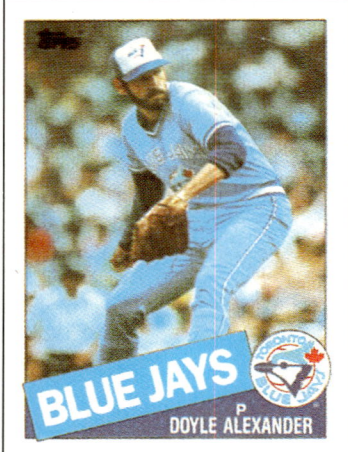

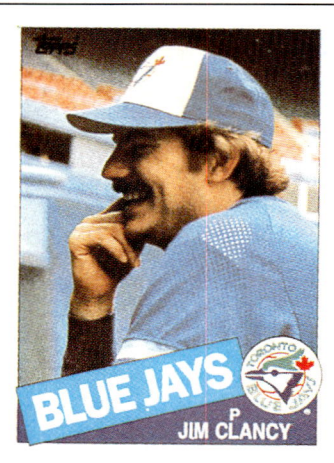
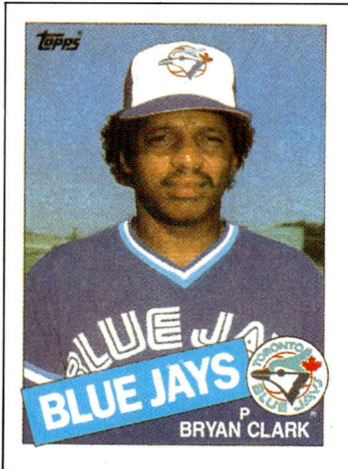
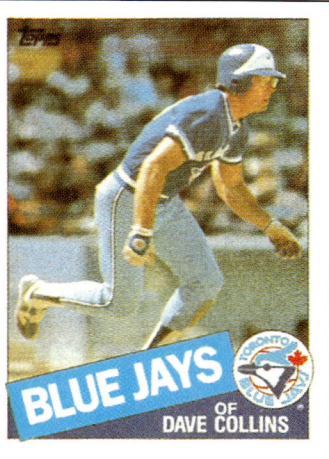
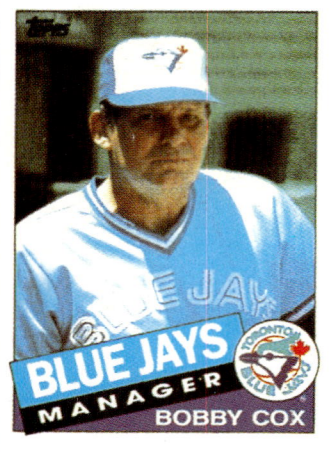

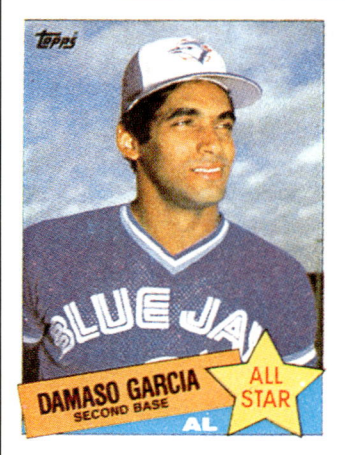
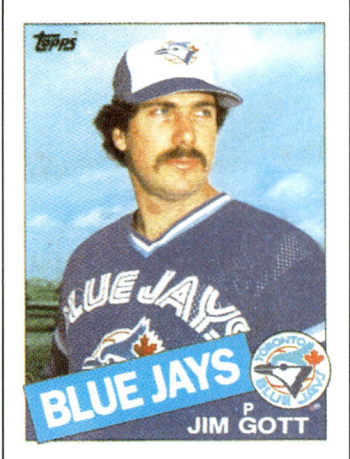

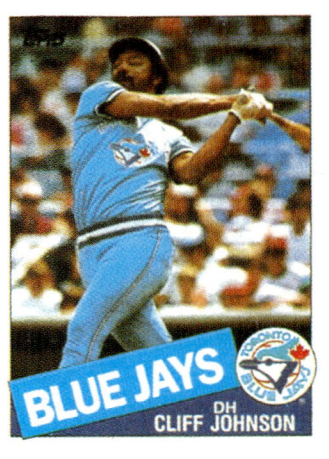

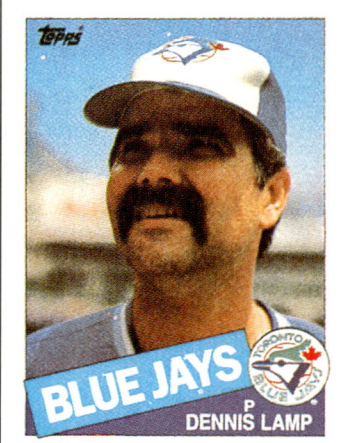

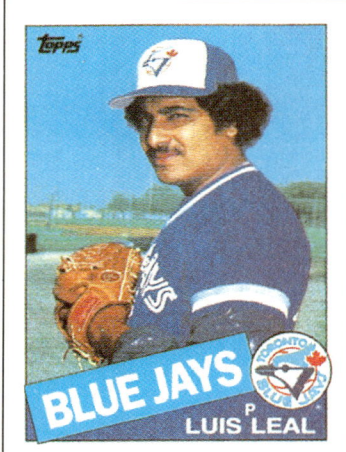

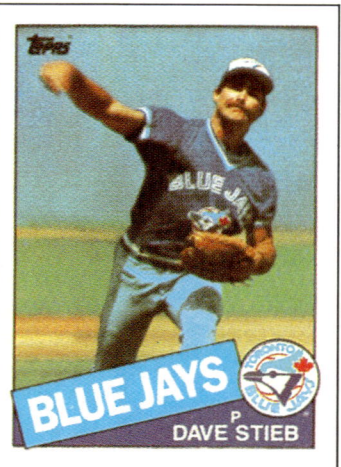

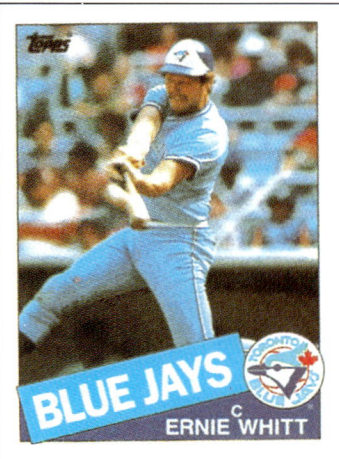

1986

Jessie Barfield and George Bell developed into perhaps the best one-two punch in the game. With Barfield and Bell frequently belting baseballs for long distances — their 71 home runs were more than any other pair of teamates in the majors — the Blue Jays scored 809 runs, second most in the majors. Barfield led everybody with 40 homers (a Toronto record) and also set team marks with his 108 RBIs (tied with Bell), 107 runs scored and .559 slugging percentage (second highest in the majors). Alas, the rightfielder, who hit .289, also set one more team record — he struck out 146 times. Bell made noise with his 31 homers, .309 average and 101 runs scored.

Despite this dynamic duo, the Blue Jays were unable to successfully defend their A.L. East title. They finished fourth at 86-76, 9½ games behind the Red Sox. A doubleheader loss to Milwaukee on the final day of the season cost them third place in Jimy Williams' first year as a major league manager.

Tony Fernandez, moved from ninth in the batting order to the top spot for most of the season, responded by leading the team with a .310 average and 213 hits (third most in the majors). He scored 91 runs and stole 25 bases. Lloyd Moseby, though batting just .253, was productive in other departments (21 homers, 86 RBIs, 89 runs, 32 steals).

Dave Stieb had difficulty throwing an effective slider for most of the season and started out by winning only two of his first 12 decisions. He finished 7-12 with a 4.74 ERA. The Blue Jays had three 14-game winners in Jimmy Key (14-11, 3.57 ERA), Jim Clancy (14-14, 3.94) and rookie Mark Eichhorn (14-6, 1.72). Eichhorn was a non-roster player who wasn't supposed to make the team but wound up as the best rookie pitcher in the league. Used mostly in middle relief, he struck out 166 batters in 157 innings. His mate in the bullpen, Tom Henke, also liked the strikeout — getting 118 in 91⅓ innings. Henke had a team-record 27 saves (third most in the league), a 9-5 record and 3.35 ERA.

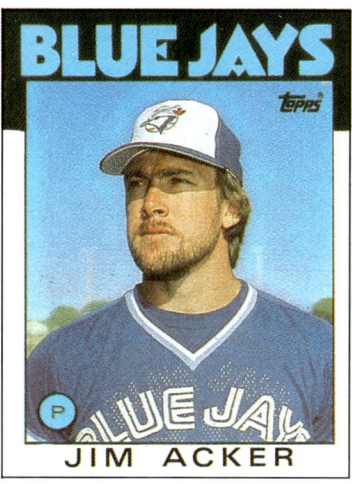
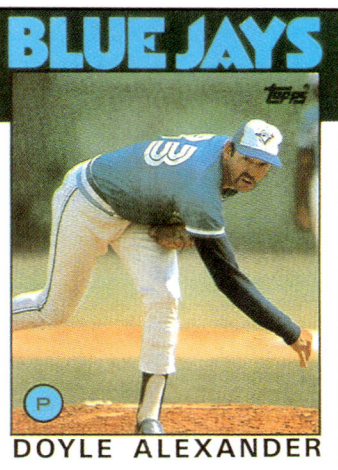
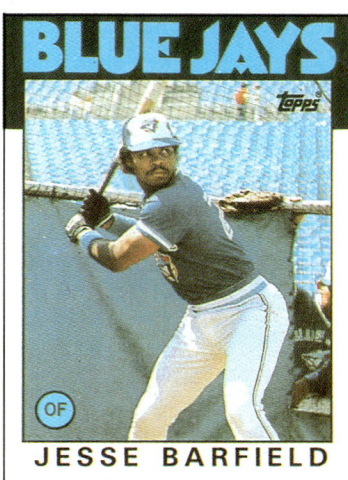

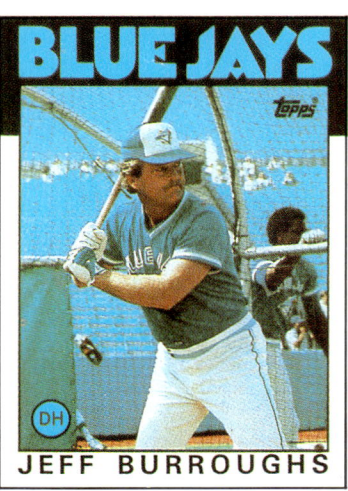

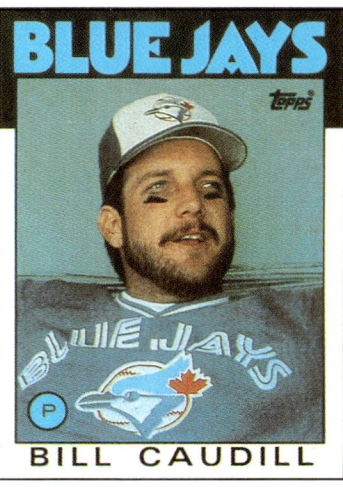

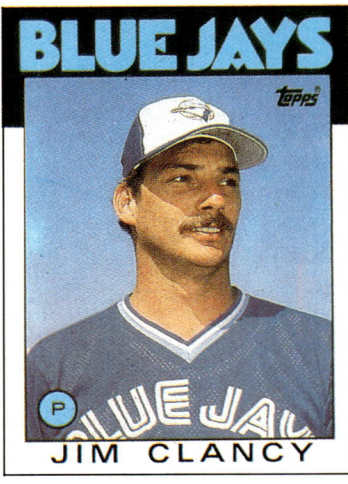
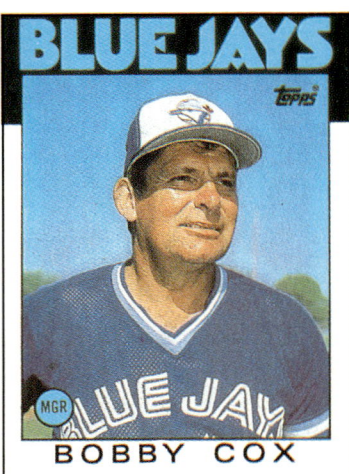

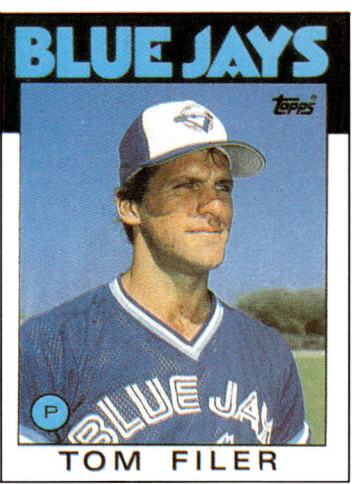

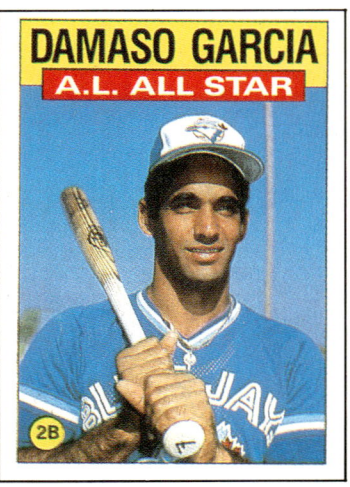
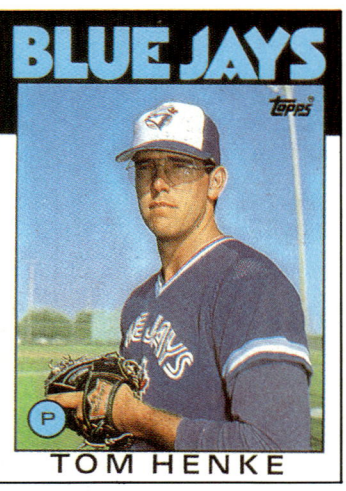
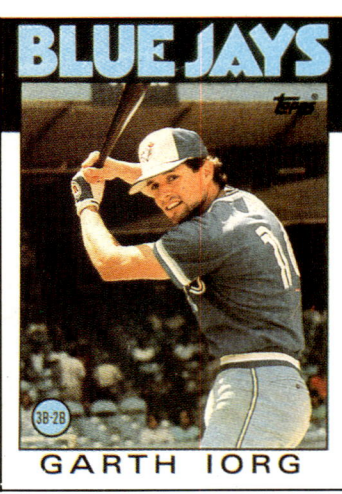

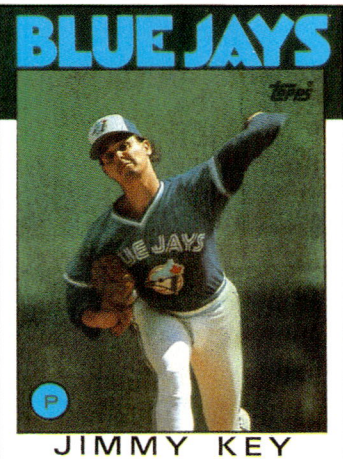

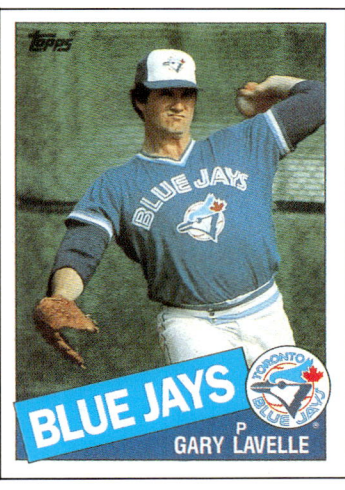
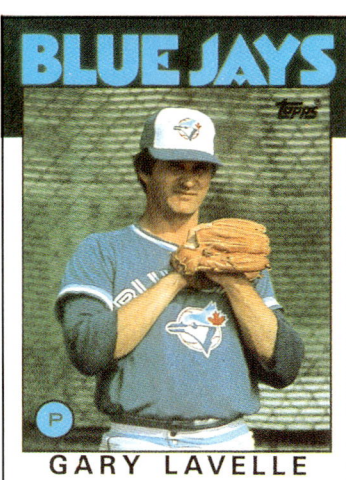
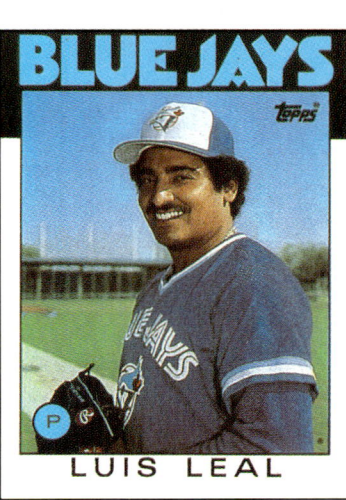
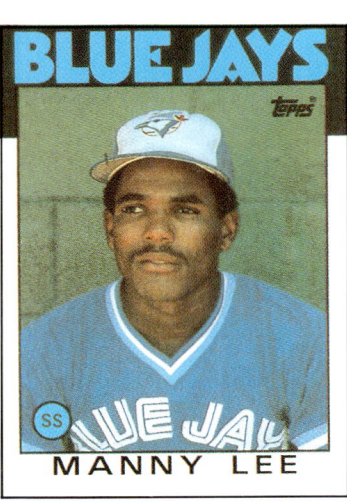

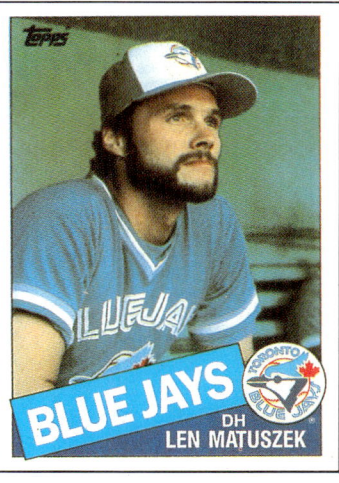

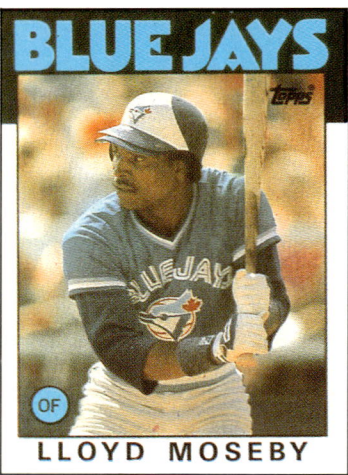

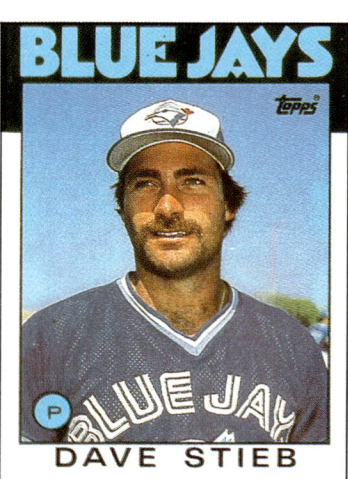

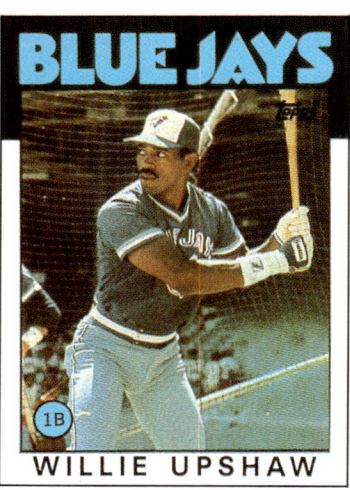

1987

Despite a heart-wrenching finish that cost them the division crown, the Toronto Blue Jays had to look at 1987 as a successful season.

Two critical injuries threw the Jays into a final-week tailspin as both shortstop Tony Fernandez and catcher Ernie Whitt were sidelined during the seven-game losing streak that closed the season.

George Bell was one of the Blue Jays who had a spectacular season, winning the American League Most Valuable Player award. Bell hit .308, was second in the league with 47 home runs and batted in a league-high 134 runs.

Bell's outfield partners — Jesse Barfield and Lloyd Moseby — also had fine seasons, although Barfield was slowed by nagging injuries that were corrected with off-season surgery. Barfield hit .263 with 28 homers and 84 RBI while Moseby batted .282 with 26 homers and 96 RBI.

Two Toronto pitchers also had sensational years. Lefthander Jimmy Key led the league's pitchers in ERA (2.76) and had a 17-8 record. Tom Henke led the league's best bullpen with 34 saves.

Mark Eichhorn, who was 10-6, and Jeff Musselman, who finished 12-5, were the other standouts in the bullpen.

Righthander Jim Clancy (15-11) led the Blue Jays with 37 starts while southpaw John Cerutti (11-4) and veteran Dave Steib (13-9) were the other regular starters for manager Jimy Williams.

In the infield, Willie Upshaw had 15 homers as a part-time first baseman and lefthanded designated hitter. Young Fred McGriff did even better in the same roles with 20 homers. Cecil Fielder was the righthanded part of this trio and had 14 home runs. Among them, the three totaled 133 RBI.

Garth Iorg and Manny Lee were the regulars at second until Fernandez was hurt and Lee moved to short. Then rookie Nelson Liriano filled in at second.

Toronto hovered around the top of the division all season until making a move in early September that boosted the Jays into first. The lead was 3½ games going into the final week before the injuries set in and the Jays were finally eliminated on the season's last day in a 1-0 loss at Detroit.

Fernandez hit .322 and his absence in the field during the final week handicapped the Jays as did the loss of Whitt, who had 19 homers for the year.

Third baseman Rance Mulliniks batted .310 to rank among the leading Blue Jays hitters for the season, although he alternated with Kelly Gruber at third.

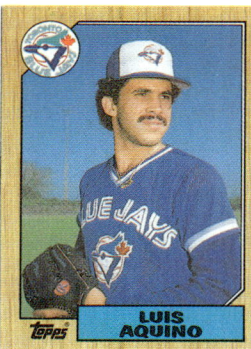

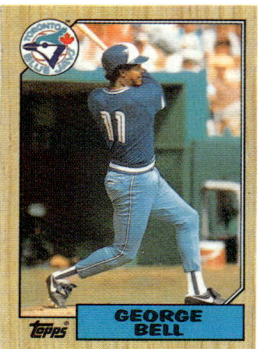

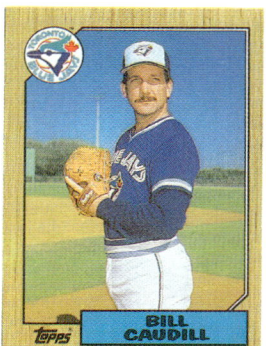

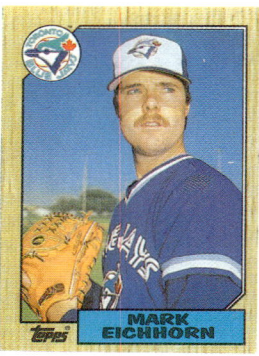

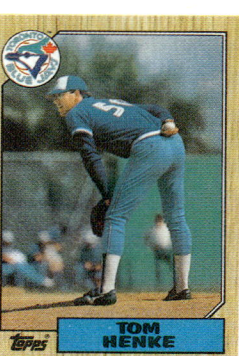
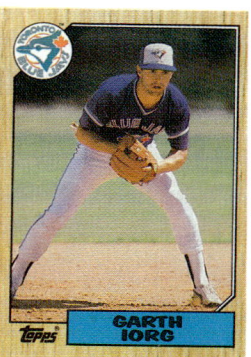

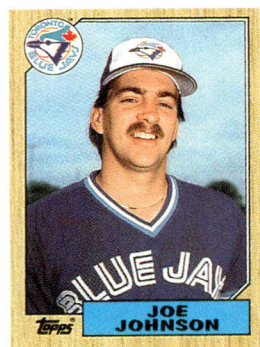
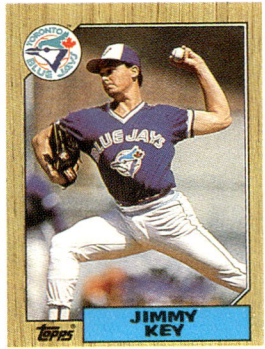
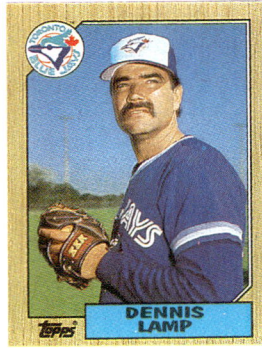

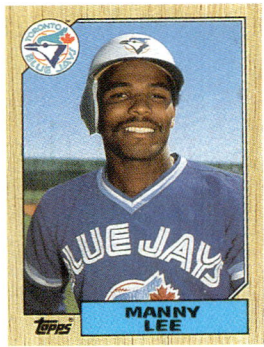

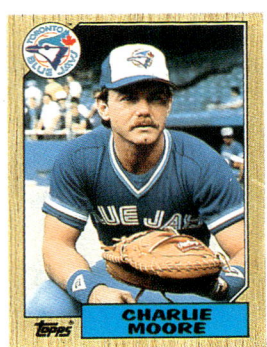
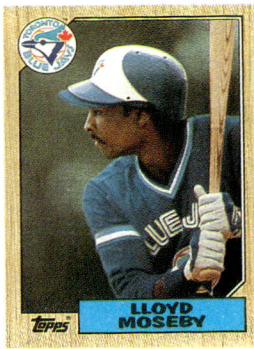

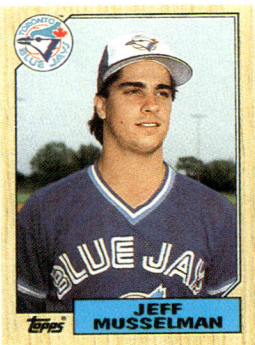
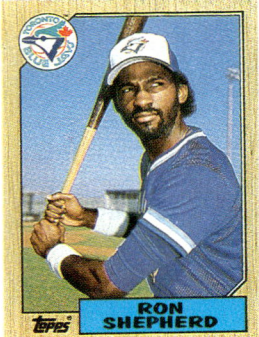

1988

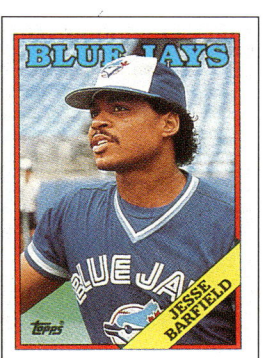 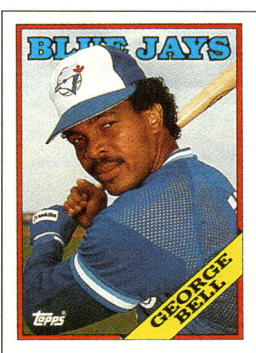 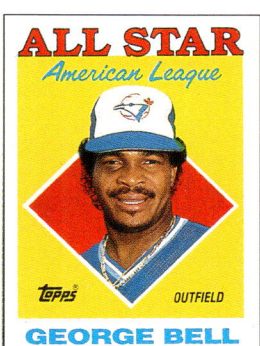 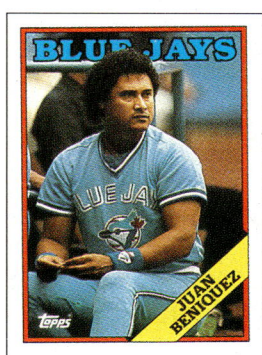

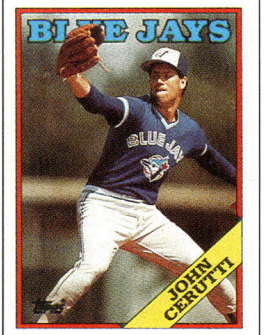  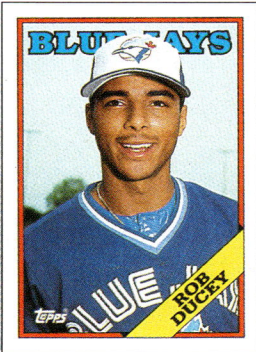 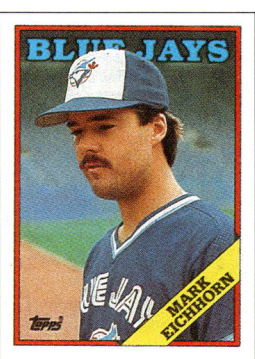

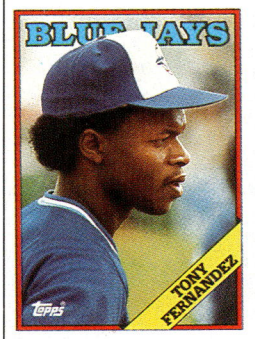  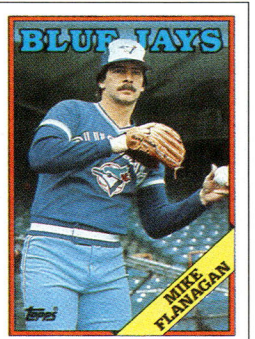 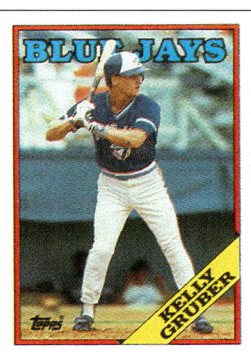

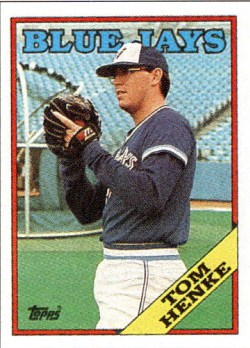
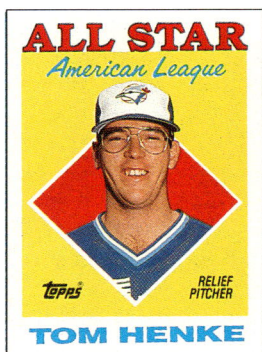
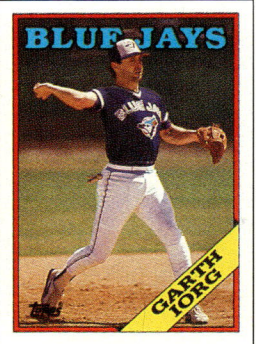

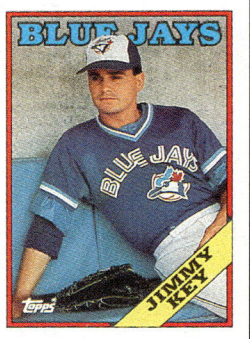
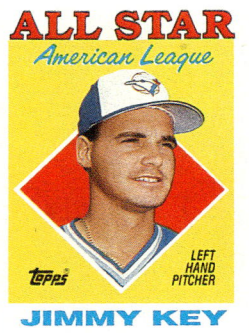
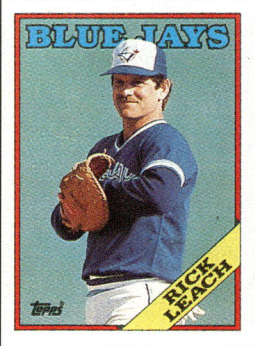
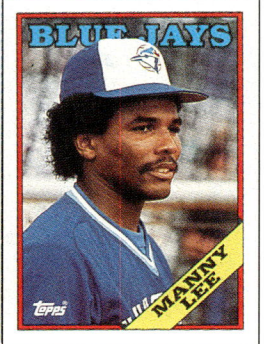
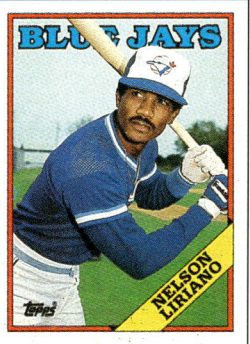
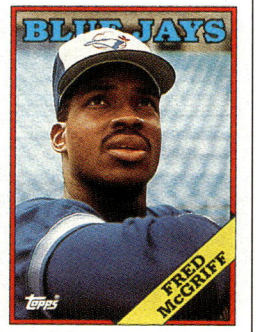

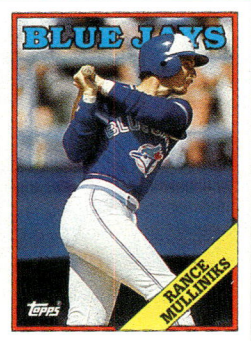
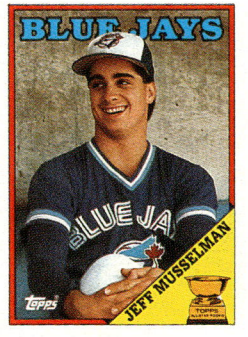
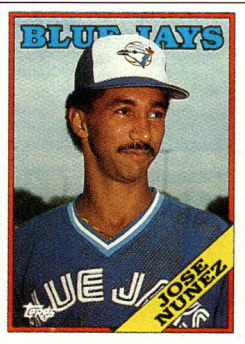
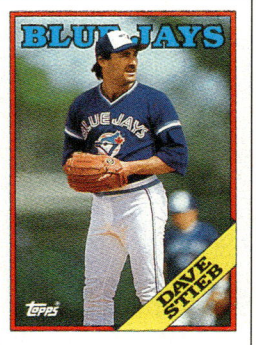

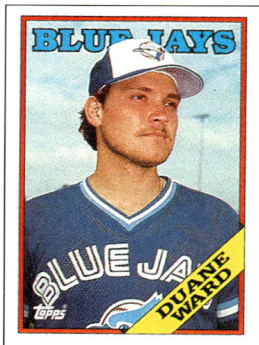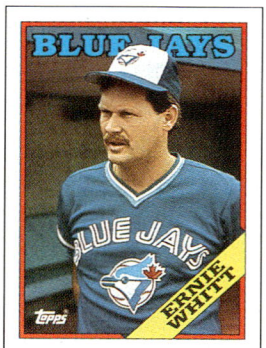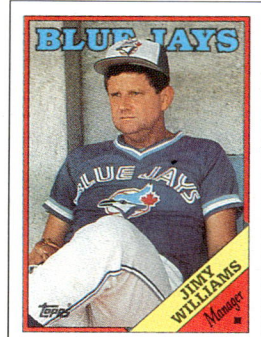

COLLECTORS CORNER

1951: Blue Back of Johnny Mize (50) lists for $25 . . . Red Back of Duke Snider (38) lists for $18 . . . Complete set of 9 Team Cards lists for $900 . . . Complete set of 11 Connie Mack All-Stars lists for $2750 with Babe Ruth and Lou Gehrig listing for $700 each . . . Current All-Stars of Jim Konstanty, Robin Roberts and Eddie Stanky list for $4000 each . . . Complete set lists for $14,250.

1952: Mickey Mantle (311) is unquestionably the most sought-after post-war gum card, reportedly valued at $6,500-plus . . . Ben Chapman (391) is photo of Sam Chapman . . . Complete set lists in excess of $36,000.

1953: Mickey Mantle (82) and Willie Mays (244) list for $1,500 each . . . Set features first TOPPS card of Hall-of-Famer Whitey Ford (207) and only TOPPS card of Hall-of-Famer Satchel Paige (220). Pete Runnels (219) is photo of Don Johnson . . . Complete set lists for $9,500.

1954: Ted Williams is depicted on two cards (1 and 250) . . . Set features rookie cards of Hank Aaron (128), Ernie Banks (94) and Al Kaline (201) . . . Card of Aaron lists for $650 . . . Card of Willie Mays (90) lists for $200 . . . Complete set lists for $5,500.

1955: Set features rookie cards of Sandy Koufax (123), Harmon Killebrew (124) and Roberto Clemente (164) . . . The Clemente and Willie Mays (194) cards list for $425 each . . . Complete set lists for $3,900.

1956: Set features rookie cards of Hall-of-Famers Will Harridge (1), Warren Giles (2), Walter Alston (8) and Luis Aparicio (292) . . . Card of Mickey Mantle (135) lists for $650 . . . Card of Willie Mays (130) lists for $125 . . . Complete set lists for $4,000 . . . The Team Cards are found both dated (1955) and undated and are valued at $15 (dated) and more . . . There are two unnumbered Checklist Cards valued high.

1957: Set features rookie cards of Don Drysdale (18), Frank Robinson (35) and Brooks Robinson (328) . . . A reversal of photo negative made Hank Aaron (20) appear as a left-handed batter . . . Card of Mickey Mantle (95) lists for $600 . . . Cards of Brooks Robinson and Sandy Koufax (302) list for $275 each . . . Complete set lists for $4,800.

1958: Set features first TOPPS cards of Casey Stengel (475) and Stan Musial (476) . . . Mike McCormick (37) is photo of Ray Monzant . . . Milt Bolling (188) is photo of Lou Berberet . . . Bob Smith (226) is photo of Bobby Gene Smith . . . Card of Mickey Mantle (150) lists for $400 . . . Card of Ted Williams (1) lists for $325 . . . Complete set lists for $4,800.

1959: In a notable error, Lou Burdette (440) is shown posing as a left-handed pitcher . . . Set features rookie card of Bob Gibson (514) . . . Ralph Lumenti (316) is photo of Camilo Pascual . . . Card of Gibson lists for $200 . . . Card of Mickey Mantle (10) lists for $300 . . . Complete set lists for $3,000.

1960: A run of 32 consecutively numbered rookie cards (117-148) includes the first card of Carl Yastrzemski (148) . . . J.C. Martin (346) is photo of Gary Peters . . . Gary Peters (407) is photo of J.C. Martin . . . Card of Yastrzemski lists for $150 . . . Card of Mickey Mantle (350) lists for $300 . . . Complete set lists for $2,600.

1961: The Warren Spahn All-Star (589) should have been numbered 587 . . . Set features rookie cards of Billy Williams (141) and Juan Marichal (417) . . . Dutch Dotterer (332) is photo of his brother, Tommy . . . Card of Mickey Mantle (300) lists for $200 . . . Card of Carl Yastrzemski (287) lists for $90 . . . Complete set lists for $3,600.

1962: Set includes special Babe Ruth feature (135-144) . . . some Hal Reniff cards numbered 139 should be 159 . . . Set features rookie card of Lou Brock (387) . . . Gene Freese (205) is shown posing as a left-handed batter . . . Card of Mickey Mantle (200) lists for $325 . . . Card of Carl Yastrzemski (425) lists for $125 . . . Complete set lists for $3,300.

1963: Set features rookie card of Pete Rose (537), which lists for $500-plus . . . Bob Uecker (126) is shown posing as a left-handed batter . . . Don Landrum (113) is photo of Ron Santo . . . Eli Grba (231) is photo of Ryne Duren . . . Card of Mickey Mantle (200) lists for $200 . . . Card of Lou Brock (472) lists for $75 . . . Complete set lists for $2,900.

1964: Set features rookie cards of Richie Allen (243), Tony Conigliaro (287) and Phil Niekro (541) . . . Lou Burdette is again shown posing as a left-handed pitcher . . . Bud Bloomfield (532) is photo of Jay Ward . . . Card of Pete Rose (125) lists for $150 . . . Card of Mickey Mantle (50) lists for $175 . . . Complete set lists for $1,600.

1965: Set features rookie cards of Dave Johnson (473), Steve Carlton (477) and Jim Hunter (526) . . . Lew Krausse (462) is photo of Pete Lovrich . . . Gene Freese (492) is again shown posing as a left-handed batter . . . Cards of Carlton and Pete Rose (207) list for $135 . . . Card of Mickey Mantle (350) lists for $300 . . . Complete set lists for $800.

1966: Set features rookie card of Jim Palmer (126) . . . For the third time (see 1962 and 1965) Gene Freese (319) is shown posing as a left-handed batter . . . Dick Ellsworth (447) is photo of Ken Hubbs (died February 13, 1964) . . . Card of Gaylord Perry (598) lists for $175 . . . Card of Willie McCovey (550) lists for $80 . . . Complete set lists for $2,500.

1967: Set features rookie cards of Rod Carew (569) and Tom Seaver (581) . . . Jim Fregosi (385) is shown posing as a left-handed batter . . . George Korince (72) is photo of James Brown but was later corrected on a second Korince card (526) . . . Card of Carew lists for $150 . . . Card of Maury Wills (570) lists for $65 . . . Complete set lists for $2,500.

1968: Set features rookie cards of Nolan Ryan (177) and Johnny Bench (247) . . . The special feature of The Sporting News All-Stars (361-380) includes eight players in the Hall of Fame . . . Card of Ryan lists for $135 . . . Card of Bench lists for $125 . . . Complete set lists for $1,200.

1969: Set features rookie card of Reggie Jackson (260) . . . There are two poses each for Clay Dalrymple (151) and Donn Clendenon (208) . . . Aurelio Rodriguez (653) is photo of Lenny Garcia (Angels' bat boy) . . . Card of Mickey Mantle (500) lists for $150 . . . Card of Jackson lists for $175 . . . Complete set lists for $1,200.

1970: Set features rookie cards of Vida Blue (21), Thurman Munson (189) and Bill Buckner (286) . . . Also included are two deceased players Miguel Fuentes (88) and Paul Edmondson (414) who died after cards went to press . . . Card of Johnny Bench (660) lists for $75 . . . Card of Pete Rose (580) lists for $75 . . . Complete set lists for $1,000.

1971: Set features rookie card of Steve Garvey (341) . . . the final series (644-752) is found in lesser quantity and includes rookie card (664) of three pitchers named Reynolds (Archie, Bob and Ken) . . . Card of Garvey lists for $65 . . . Card of Pete Rose (100) lists for $45 . . . Complete set lists for $1,000.

1972: There were 16 cards featuring photos of players in their boyhood years . . . Dave Roberts (91) is photo of Danny Coombs . . . Brewers Rookie Card (162) includes photos of Darrell Porter and Jerry Bell, which were reversed . . . Cards of Steve Garvey (686) and Rod Carew (695) list for $60 . . . Card of Pete Rose (559) lists for $50 . . . Complete set lists for $1,000.

1973: A special Home Run Card (1) depicted Babe Ruth, Hank Aaron and Willie Mays . . . Set features rookie card of Mike Schmidt (615) listing for $175 . . . Joe Rudi (360) is photo of Gene Tenace . . . Card of Pete Rose (130) lists for $18 . . . Card of Reggie Jackson (255) lists for $12.50 . . . Complete set lists for $600.

1974: Set features 15 San Diego Padres cards printed as "Washington, N.L." due to report of franchise move, later corrected . . . Also included was a 44-card Traded Series which updated team changes . . . Set features rookie card of Dave Winfield (456) . . . Card of Mike Schmidt (283) lists for $35 . . . Card of Winfield lists for $25 . . . Complete set lists for $325.

1975: Herb Washington (407) is the only card ever published with position "designated runner," featuring only base-running statistics . . . Set features rookie cards of Robin Yount (223), George Brett (228), Jim Rice (616), Gary Carter (620) and Keith Hernandez (623) . . . Don Wilson (455) died after cards went to press (January 5, 1975) . . . Card of Brett lists for $50 . . . Cards of Rice and Carter list for $35 . . . Complete set lists for $475 . . . TOPPS also tested the complete 660-card series in a smaller size (2¼" x 3 1/8") in certain areas of USA in a limited supply . . . Complete set of "Mini-Cards" lists for $700.

1976: As in 1974 there was a 44-card Traded Series . . . Set features five Father & Son cards (66-70) and ten All-Time All-Stars (341-350) . . . Card of Pete Rose (240) lists for $15 . . . Cards of Jim Rice (340), Gary Carter (441) and George Brett (19) list for $12 . . . Complete set lists for $225.

1977: Set features rookie cards of Andre Dawson (473) and Dale Murphy (476) . . . Reuschel Brother Combination (634) shows the two (Paul and Rick) misidentified . . . Dave Collins (431) is photo of Bob Jones . . . Card of Murphy lists for $65 . . . Card of Pete Rose (450) lists for $8.50 . . . Complete set lists for $250.

1978: Record Breakers (1-7) feature Lou Brock, Sparky Lyle, Willie McCovey, Brooks Robinson, Pete Rose, Nolan Ryan and Reggie Jackson . . . Set features rookie cards of Jack Morris (703), Lou Whitaker (704), Paul Molitor/Alan Trammell (707), Lance Parrish (708) and Eddie Murray (36) . . . Card of Murray lists for $35 . . . Card of Parrish lists for $35 . . . Complete set lists for $200.

1979: Bump Wills (369) was originally shown with Blue Jays affiliation but later corrected to Rangers . . . Set features rookie cards of Ozzie Smith (116), Pedro Guerrero (719), Lonnie Smith (722) and Terry Kennedy (724) . . . Larry Cox (489) is photo of Dave Rader . . . Card of Dale Murphy (39) lists for $8 . . . Cards of Ozzie Smith and Eddie Murray (640) list for $7.50 . . . Complete set lists for $135.

1980: Highlights (1-6) feature Hall-of-Famers Lou Brock, Carl Yastrzemski, Willie McCovey and Pete Rose . . . Set features rookie cards of Dave Stieb (77), Rickey Henderson (482) and Dan Quisenberry (667) . . . Card of Henderson lists for $28 . . . Card of Dale Murphy (274) lists for $5.50 . . . Complete set lists for $135.

1981: Set features rookie cards of Fernando Valenzuela (302), Kirk Gibson (315), Harold Baines (347) and Tim Raines (479) . . . Jeff Cox (133) is photo of Steve McCatty . . . John Littlefield (489) is photo of Mark Riggins . . . Card of Valenzuela lists for $7.50 . . . Card of Raines lists for $9 . . . Complete set lists for $80.

1982: Pascual Perez (383) printed with no position on front lists for $35, later corrected . . . Set features rookie cards of Cal Ripken (21), Jesse Barfield (203), Steve Sax (681) and Kent Hrbek (766) . . . Dave Rucker (261) is photo of Roger Weaver . . . Steve Bedrosian (502) is photo of Larry Owen . . . Card of Ripken lists for $12.50 . . . Cards of Barfield and Sax list for $5 . . . Complete set lists for $75.

1983: Record Breakers (1-6) feature Tony Armas, Rickey Henderson, Greg Minton, Lance Parrish, Manny Trillo and John Wathan . . . A series of Super Veterans features early and current photos of 34 leading players . . . Set features rookie cards of Tony Gwynn (482) and Wade Boggs (498) . . . Card of Boggs lists for $32 . . . Card of Gwynn lists for $16 . . . Complete set lists for $85.

1984: Highlights (1-6) salute eleven different players . . . A parade of superstars is included in Active Leaders (701-718) . . . Set features rookie card of Don Mattingly (8) listing for $35 . . . Card of Darryl Strawberry (182) lists for $10 . . . Complete set lists for $85.

1985: A Father & Son Feature (131-143) is again included . . . Set features rookie cards of Scott Bankhead (393), Mike Dunne (395), Shane Mack (398), John Marzano (399), Oddibe McDowell (400), Mark McGwire (401), Pat Pacillo (402), Cory Snyder (403) and Billy Swift (404) as part of salute to 1984 USA Baseball Team (389-404) that participated in Olympic Games plus rookie cards of Roger Clemens (181) and Eric Davis (627) . . . Card of McGwire lists for $20 . . . Card of Davis lists for $18 . . . Card of Clemens lists for $11 . . . Complete set lists for $95.

1986: Set includes Pete Rose Feature (2-7), which reproduces each of Rose's TOPPS cards from 1963 thru 1985 (four per card) . . . Bob Rodgers (141) should have been numbered 171 . . . Ryne Sandberg (690) is the only card with TOPPS logo omitted . . . Complete set lists for $24.

1987: Record Breakers (1-7) feature Roger Clemens, Jim Deshaies, Dwight Evans, Davey Lopes, Dave Righetti, Ruben Sierra and Todd Worrell . . . Jim Gantner (108) is shown with Brewers logo reversed . . . Complete set lists for $22.

1988: Record Breakers (1-7) include Vince Coleman, Don Mattingly, Mark McGwire, Eddie Murray, Phil & Joe Niekro, Nolan Ryan and Benny Santiago. Al Leiter (18) was originally shown with photo of minor leaguer Steve George and later corrected. Complete set lists for $20.00.

Pitching Record & Index

PLAYER	G	IP	W	L	R	ER	SO	BB	GS	CG	SHO	SV	ERA
ACKER, JIM	175	411	20	20	207	182	188	154	27	0	0	12	3.99
ALEXANDER, DOYLE	467	2708.1	160	135	1228	1117	1199	803	370	82	13	0	3.71
AQUINO, LUIS	7	11.1	1	1	8	8	5	3	0	0	0	0	6.35
BARLOW, MIKE	133	247	10	6			96	104	2	0	0	6	4.63
BERENGUER, JUAN	183	645	30	41	324	287	498	335	86	5	2	5	4.00
BOMBACK, MARK	74	314.2	16	18			124	110	45	4	0	0	4.46
BRUNO, TOM	69	123	7	7			80	61	4	0	0	1	4.24
BUSKEY, TOM	258	480	21	27			212	167	0	0	0	34	3.66
BYRD, JEFF	17	87	2	13			40	68	17	1	0	0	6.21
CAUDILL, BILL	439	659.1	35	52	289	265	612	287	24	1	0	105	3.62
CERUTTI, JOHN	38	152	9	6	80	71	94	51	21	2	1	0	4.20
CLANCY, JIM	279	1768.1	102	116	895	812	939	687	277	64	10	0	4.13
CLARK, BRYAN	158	478.1	18	23			243	241	37	4	1	4	4.23
COLEMAN, JOE H.	484	2571	142	135			1728	1003	340	94	18	7	3.69
COOPER, DON	37	75.2		6			43	43	3	0	0	0	5.23
CRUZ, VICTOR	187	271	18	23			248	131	0	0	0	37	3.02
EDGE, BUTCH	9	52	3	4			19	24	9	1	0	0	5.19
EICHORN, MARK	76	195	14	9	60	53	182	59	7	0	0	10	2.45
ESPINOSA, NINO	139	820	44	55			338	252	130	24	5	0	4.16
FILER, TOM	19	89.1	8	2			39	36	17	0	0	0	4.63
FLANAGAN, MIKE	328	2090	136	103	966	892	1175	656	311	94	17	4	3.84
FREISLEBEN, DAVE	202	866	34	60			430	430	121	17	6	4	4.29
GARVIN, JERRY	196	607.1	20	41			320	219	65	15	1	8	4.42
GEISEL, DAVE	119	181.1	7	5			127	82	8	0	0	2	3.67
GOTT, JIM	125	570.2	28	40			354	234	91	10	3	2	4.31
GRILLI, STEVE	70	148	4	3			91	96	2	0	0	3	4.50
HARGAN, STEVE	354	1631	87	107			891	614	215	56	17	17	3.92
HARTENSTEIN, CHUCK	187	297	17	19			135	89	0	0	0	23	4.39
HENKE, TOM	132	191.1	15	9	80	71	211	72	0	0	0	43	3.34
HUFFMAN, PHIL	31	173	6	18			56	68	31	2	1	0	5.77
JACKSON, ROY LEE	280	559.1	28	34	260	234	351	203	18	1	0	34	3.77
JEFFERSON, JESSE	237	1086	39	81			522	520	144	25	4	1	4.81
JOHNSON, JERRY	365	771	48	51			489	389	39	7	2	41	4.31
KEY, JIMMY	134	506.2	32	22	212	195	270	156	67	7	2	10	3.46
KIRKWOOD, DON	120	375	18	23			194	135	37	7	0	3	4.37
KUCEK, JACK	59	207	7	16			121	111	27	3	0	0	5.09
LAMP, DENNIS	396	1353.2	74	76	670	587	590	411	157	21	7	33	3.90
LAVELLE, GARY	716	1053.1	78	74			746	418	3	0	0	135	2.84
LEAL, LUIS	165	946.2	51	58			491	320	151	27	3	0	4.14
LEMANCZYK, DAVE	185	912	37	63			429	363	103	30	3	1	4.63
LEMONGELLO, MARK	89	537	22	38			209	159	74	17	1	1	4.06
LUEBBER, STEVE	66	206	6	10			93	106	24	2	1	1	4.63
MCLAUGHLIN, JOEY	250	449	29	28			268	198	12	0	0	36	3.85
MILLER, DYAR	251	466	23	17			235	177	1	0	0	3	3.23
MIRABELLA, PAUL	156	316.1	11	24			163	161	31	3	1	7	4.92
MOFFITT, RANDY	534	782	43	52			455	286	1	0	0	96	3.65
MOORE, BALOR	180	719	28	48			496	365	98	16	4	1	4.52
MORGAN, MIKE	101	507	21	45	302	277	228	237	78	14	1	1	4.92
MURPHY, TOM	439	1443	68	101			621	493	147	22	2	59	3.78
MURRAY, DALE	514	898	53	50			400	329	1	0	0	60	3.82
NIEKRO, PHIL	838	5265	311	261	2238	1915	3278	1743	690	243	45	29	3.27
SCHROM, KEN	144	746.1	45	38	409	370	311	263	108	18	2	1	4.46
SINGER, BILL	322	2174	118	127			1515	781	308	96	24	2	3.39
STIEB, DAVE	259	1859.1	102	92	773	690	1069	631	254	85	21	1	3.34

PLAYER	G	IP	W	L	R	ER	SO	BB	GS	CG	SHO	SV	ERA
TODD, JACKSON	64	287	10	16			138	88	36	7	0	0	4.39
UNDERWOOD, TOM	379	1586.1	86	87			948	662	203	35	6	18	3.89
VUCKOVICH, PETE	280	1422	91	65			870	534	180	38	8	10	3.68
WARD, DUANE	12	18	0	2	17	16	9	12	1	0	0	0	8.00
WILLIS, MIKE	144	296	7	21			149	124	6	1	0	15	4.59

Batting Record & Index

PLAYER	G	AB	R	H	2B	3B	HR	RBI	SB	SLG	BB	SO	AVG
ADAMS, GLENN	661	1617	152	452	79	5	34	225	6	.398	111	183	.280
AIKENS, WILLIE	762	2472	299	671	124	2	109	410	3	.456	317	438	.271
AINGE, DANNY	211	665	57	146	19	4	2	37	12	.269	37	128	.220
ALLENSON, GARY	402	1027	112	231	48	2	19	128	3	.331	130	182	.225
ASHBY, ALAN	1150	3449	321	835	156	12	69	414	7	.354	375	525	.242
AULT, DOUG	256	713	66	168	29	5	17	86	4	.362	71	108	.236
BAILOR, BOB	955	2937	339	775	107	23	9	222	90	.325	187	164	.264
BARFIELD, JESSE	715	2325	371	634	112	19	128	376	45	.502	238	578	.273
BEAMON, CHARLIE JR	37	36	7	7	1	0	0	0	0	.222	1	6	.194
BELL, GEORGE	574	2129	297	610	112	21	92	319	43	.488	117	282	.287
BENIQUEZ, JUAN	1377	4338	581	1193	176	29	70	421	104	.377	325	507	.275
BONNELL, BARRY	959	3017	359	823	141	24	56	351	64	.391	228	374	.273
BOSETTI, RICK	445	1543	172	385	70	30	37	133	30	.327	79	188	.250
BRAUN, STEVE	1425	3650	466	989	155	19	52	388	45	.367	579	433	.271
BROWN, BOBBY	502	1277	183	313	38	12	26	130	4	.355	94	238	.245
BURROUGHS, JEFF	1689	5536	720	1443	230	20	240	882	16	.439	831	1135	.261
CANNON, JOE	148	227	34	40	3	1	0	11	5	.211	15	54	.176
CARTY, RICO	1651	5606	712	1677	278	17	204	890	21	.464	642	663	.299
CERONE, RICK	858	2796	266	665	126	12	43	304	4	.338	198	290	.238
COLLINS, DAVE	1368	4484	612	1231	171	50	32	344	369	.356	422	594	.275
COX, BOBBY	220	628	50	141	22	2	9	58	3	.309	75	126	.225
COX, TED	272	771	65	189	29	1	10	79	3	.324	57	98	.245
DAVIS, BOB J.E.	290	665	60	131	19	3	6	51	7	.262	40	118	.197
DAVIS, DICK	403	1217	160	323	62	7	27	141	13	.394	50	151	.265
EWING, SAM	167	361	31	92	11	3	6	47	1	.352	28	65	.255
FAIRLY, RON	2442	7184	931	1913	307	33	215	1044	35	.408	1052	877	.266
FERNANDEZ, TONY	427	1518	196	448	70	23	15	137	43	.401	89	110	.295
FIELDER, CECIL	64	157	13	36	6	0	4	29	0	.420	12	40	.229
GARCIA, DAMASO	931	3651	461	1046	173	26	32	301	197	.374	112	292	.286
GARCIA, PEDRO	558	1797	196	395	89	15	37	184	35	.348	102	329	.220
GOMEZ, LUIS	609	1251	108	263	26	5	0	90	6	.239	86	129	.210
GRIFFIN, ALFREDO	1228	4408	501	1133	160	63	19	336	135	.335	194	391	.257
GRUBER, KELLY	107	172	21	32	4	1	6	18	5	.326	5	35	.186
HARTSFIELD, ROY	265	976	138	266	30	7	13	59	14	.358	73	146	.273
HEARRON, JEFF	16	30	2	6	1	0	0	4	0	.233	4	9	.200
HORTON, WILLIE	2028	7298	873	1993	284	40	325	1163	20	.457	620	1313	.273
HOWELL, ROY	1112	3791	422	991	183	31	80	454	9	.389	318	674	.261
HUTTON, TOM	952	1655	196	410	63	7	22	186	15	.334	234	140	.248
IORG, GARTH	809	2140	216	568	114	16	16	208	20	.356	93	246	.265
JOHNSON, CLIFF	1369	3945	539	1016	198	10	196	699	9	.462	568	719	.258
JOHNSON, TIM	516	1269	116	283	27	13	0	84	18	.265	88	231	.223
KELLY, D. PAT	3	7	0	2	0	0	0	0	0	.286	0	4	.286
KLUTTS, MICKEY	199	536	49	129	26	1	4	59	1	.315	34	101	.241
KUSICK, CRAIG	497	1238	155	291	50	3	46	171	1	.392	194	228	.235
LEACH, RICK	426	912	102	234	47	7	12	96	6	.363	80	112	.257
LEE, MANNY	99	118	17	24	0	1	1	7	1	.246	6	19	.203
MACHA, KEN	180	380	37	98	16	3	1	35	0	.324	39	68	.258
MARTINEZ, BUCK	968	2583	232	589	120	10	56	309	5	.347	210	394	.228
MASON, JIM	633	1584	140	322	53	12	12	114	2	.275	124	316	.203
MATUSZEK, LEN	363	805	113	191	40	5	30	119	6	.411	87	164	.237
MAYBERRY, JOHN	1620	5447	733	1379	211	18	255	879	20	.439	881	810	.253
McKAY, DAVE	645	1928	191	441	70	15	21	170	2	.313	86	337	.229
MILNER, BRIAN	2	9	3	4	0	0	0	2	0	.667	0	1	.444
MOORE, CHARLIE	1283	3926	441	1029	177	42	35	401	51	.355	333	458	.262
MOSEBY, LLOYD	974	3558	513	928	173	46	102	471					

PLAYER	G	AB	R	H	2B	3B	HR	RBI	SB	SLG	BB	SO	AVG
MULLINIKS, RANCE	822	2288	295	614	150	12	43	273	11	.401	269	340	.268
NICOSIA, STEVE	352	923	86	229	52	3	11	87	5	.347	86	90	.248
NORDBROOK, TIM	128	169	27	30	1	1	0	3	4	.195	25	26	.178
NORDHAGEN, WAYNE	502	1423	147	401	77	8	39	205	1	.429	54	162	.282
OLIVER, AL	2368	9049	1189	2743	529	77	219	1326	84	.451	535	756	.303
ORTA, JORGE	1734	5779	730	1610	263	63	128	741	79	.412	497	707	.279
PETRALLI, GENO	136	288	27	78	13	3	2	30	3	.358	18	33	.271
POWELL, HOSKEN	594	1816	241	470	78	17	17	161	39	.349	144	164	.259
RADER, DOUG	1465	5186	631	1302	245	39	155	722	37	.403	528	1057	.251
RAMOS, DOMINGO	250	517	50	108	16	0	3	33	5	.257	42	67	.209
REVERING, DAVE	557	1832	205	486	83	5	62	234	6	.430	148	240	.265
ROBERTS, LEON	901	2737	342	731	126	28	78	328	26	.419	256	428	.267
ROBERTSON, BOB	829	2385	283	578	93	10	115	368	7	.434	317	546	.242
ROOF, PHIL	857	2151	190	463	69	13	43	210	11	.319	184	504	.215
SCOTT, JOHN	118	257	35	57	9	2	2	15	13	.280	6	45	.222
SHEPHERD, RON	115	108	23	18	6	0	2	5	13	.278	5	37	.167
SOLAITA, TONY	525	1316	164	336	66	1	50	203	2	.421	214	345	.255
STAGGS, STEVE	119	369	47	94	13	8	1	28	7	.350	55	55	.255
THORNTON, LOU	56	72	18	17	1	1	0	8	7	.319	2	24	.236
TORRES, HECTOR	622	1738	148	375	46	7	18	115	7	.281	104	229	.216
UPSHAW, WILLIE	965	3198	470	857	155	38	97	420	66	.431	332	496	.268
VELEZ, OTTO	637	1802	244	452	87	11	78	272	6	.441	336	414	.251
WARNER, HARRY							No major league statistics						
WEBSTER, MITCH	266	822	132	232	41	16	19	83	51	.440	79	119	.282
WELLS, BOOMER	47	127	12	29	6	2	0	8	0	.173	6	20	.228
WHITT, ERNIE	835	2303	266	571	107	11	86	323	13	.416	248	312	.248
WILBORN, TED	30	20	5	2	0	0	0	1	0	.100	1	8	.100
WILLIAMS, JIMY	14	13	1	3	0	0	0	0	0	.231	1	6	.231
WOODS, ALVIS	586	1958	228	529	97	14	33	188	23	.385	164	175	.270
WOODS, GARY	525	1032	117	251	50	4	13	110	19	.337	86	187	.243